Robin Waterfield graduated from Manchester University in 1974. He went on to four years of research at King's College, Cambridge, into Greek philosophy, especially Plato. There followed four years as a university lecturer in ancient Greek, but he now finds himself self-employed as a writer and editor. A number of his translations of Greek philosophical texts are published by Penguin Classics: Plato: *Philebus*, Plato: *Theaetetus*, and (in the volume *Early Socratic Dialogues*) Plato: *Hippias Major*, *Hippias Minor* and *Euthydemus*. A translation of Xenophon's Socratic writings is forthcoming in 1989.

Keith Critchlow, architect, scholar, and geometer, is a graduate of the Royal College of Art, London. His published works include *Order in Space*, *Islamic Patterns: An Analytic and Cosmological Approach*, *The Soul as Sphere and Androgyne*, and *Time Stands Still: New Light on Megalithic Science*. He has lectured in Europe, Asia, Africa, Iran, and the United States.

**Other translations
by Robin Waterfield:**

Plato: *Philebus*
Penguin Books, 1982

Plato: *Theatetus*
Penguin Books, 1987

Plato: *Early Socratic Dialogues*
Penguin Books, 1987
with T.J. Saunders, *et al.*

Xenophon: *Conversations
of Socrates*
Penguin Books, 1989
with H. Tredennick

THE THEOLOGY
OF
ARITHMETIC

On the Mystical, Mathematical
and Cosmological Symbolism
of the First Ten Numbers

Attributed to Iamblichus

TRANSLATED FROM THE GREEK BY
ROBIN WATERFIELD

WITH A FOREWORD BY
KEITH CRITCHLOW

A Kairos Book

PHANES PRESS
1988

B
669
.Z7
I1713
1988

Published by Phanes Press, PO Box 6114, Grand Rapids, Michigan 49516, USA.

Designed by David R. Fideler
Printed and bound in the United States

This book is printed on alkaline paper which conforms to the permanent paper standard developed by the National Information Standards Organization.

Library of Congress Cataloging-in-Publication Data

Iamblichus, ca. 250-ca. 330
    [Theological principles of arithmetic. English]
    The theology of arithmetic: on the mystical, mathematical and cosmological symbolism of the first ten numbers / attributed to Iamblichus; translated from the Greek by Robin Waterfield; with a foreword by Keith Critchlow.
        p. cm.
    Translation of: Theological principles of arithmetic.
    Bibliography: p.
    ISBN 0-933999-71-2 (alk. paper). ISBN 0-933999-72-0 (pbk.: alk paper).
    1. Symbolism of numbers—Early works to 1800. 2. Pythagoras and Pythagorean school—Early works to 1800. I. Waterfield, Robin A. H. II. Title.
B669.Z7I1713 1988
119—dc19   88-23012
                                                                          CIP

To Pythagoras
who taught that for health, art and science are inseparable

"By him that gave to our generation the Tetraktys, which
contains the fount and root of eternal nature"
(Pythagorean oath)

and to Steve Lee, reluctant arithmologist

Contents

Foreword

Kairos is privileged to present this timely translation of *The Theology of Arithmetic*, and is most grateful to Robin Waterfield for his dedicated and scholarly translation. We offer the following observations to emphasize the inner nature of a document like this, which invites interpretation.

Aetius (first or second century A.D.) is one of the most important sources for the opinions of the earliest Greek philosophers, whose actual works have for the most part perished. He says of Pythagoras (I.3.8) that he was the first to call the search for wisdom "philosophy," and that he "assumed as first principles the numbers and the symmetries existing among them, which he calls harmonies, and the elements compounded of both, that are called geometrical. And," Aetius continues, "he says that the nature of Number is the Decad." However 'unreliable' we choose to treat this transmission, even this brief extract does contain some remarkably significant possibilities which call for interpretation.

That numbers were assumed as first principles is not unexpected, but the idea of "symmetries existing among them" is particularly evocative. Their harmonies are likewise said to be among them. Further, the geometricals are elements compounded of the numbers *with* their inherent symmetrical harmonies. The progression given by Aetius is from first principles to numbers, symmetries, harmonies and geometricals, and it seems to reflect the progression arithmetic, harmonic and geometric, which are the three primary means that Plato proposed that the Divine Artificer (*demiurgos*) used to proportion the 'world soul' (*Timaeus* 36).

Finally, that "the nature of Number is the Decad" could place quite a different perspective on the issues that took up so much of Aristotle's time, as he chewed over the paradox of the linear generation of the 'incomparable' ideal numbers. The indication is that the Decad is both complete and is the essential nature of all number—a monad of minimum ten. That ten is 'complete at four' is a well-known Pythagorean paradox based on the simple cumulative progression of 1+2+3+4=10; or, in the direct manner of those who had no separate number symbols:

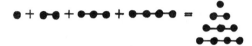

Figure 1

However, there is obviously an allegorical reasoning which allows paradox to play a free part in the 'generation' or simultaneous 'being' of the first nine (or ten) ideal numbers. Given that Aetius' ultimate source is Theophrastus, who wrote in the fourth century B.C. the *Doctrines of Natural Philosophers* (*Phusikon Doxai*), then we have a most interesting Pythagorean idea to contend with—that ideal number is not necessarily subject to a sequential or causal progression from one through to ten, but is rather a unity with ten essential and potential qualities, simultaneously present in the Decad or Tetraktys.

Although it is well known that numbers traditionally come 'before' bodies, there is the possibility of understanding the shadow allegory of Plato's Cave in terms of the number points, which we might call 'dots,' representing 'incomparable sets' of one dot for oneness, two dots for duality, three dots for triplicity, four dots for quaternity, and so on. In this case, the 'shadows' would work in reverse, as it were. From the pure, indescribable light of unity, the first visual evidence, we might say, is for the units to become surface 'dots,' which eventually become matter as spheres, i.e. projecting into the dimensions.

In this way we can see a progression that embraces Plato's doctrine that 'images' in the human mind reflect the universal source in the mind of the Divine Artificer. So we get One reflecting as a single dot or shadow on a surface for us to 'imagine' or remember Oneness from. If we should take the Pythagorean tradition literally, the first and comprehensive evidence of 'ideal' or archetypal number is an array of 'dots' in triangular form:

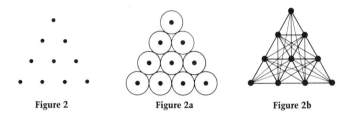

Figure 2   **Figure 2a**   **Figure 2b**

Figure 2. The Pythagorean Tetraktys as 'dots.'
Figure 2a. The Pythagorean Tetraktys as close packed circles in triangular form.
Figure 2b. The Tetraktys of ten 'dots' with the basic symmetries between them.

This pattern might be called, in current usage, a refraction pattern of a single triangle. It is important to remember that the ancient Greeks did not have an abstract system of number symbols, and used the letters of their alphabet as number symbols. They also commonly manipulated pebbles to learn arithmetic and used these small stones on calculating boards. In this case, number *patterns* were their common experience of arithmetic. From this use of pebbles, we have inherited the word 'calculation,' from the Latin *calculus*, which means 'pebble.'

This Decad or pattern can be taken both as a graphic (differentiated) form of ten dots in four rows and/or as *one* triangular form outlined in nine dots with a center point. In terms of the Platonic formula for knowledge of any object (see the Platonic *Seventh Letter*), this would be the second stage of definition.

From the above pattern, we can see how the Tetraktys of the Pythagoreans may represent both a minimal oneness *and* a maximal tenness simultaneously. The Pythagoreans must have based their deep regard for this particular form (see the Pythagorean oath quoted on the dedication page) on the breadth and depth of symbolism it carried or could carry for them.

The doctrine of the essentiality of number, which has held so much inspirational power for so long (and is hardly far from modern concepts of mathematical atomism) is (a) unlikely to have been totally divulged in the literature and is (b) likely to have had more than one teaching related to it. Yet this multiplicity of teaching, that inevitably leads to paradox,[1] is not necessarily a helpful ingredient during the time of nurturing dialectic and logic in a developing philosopher; there was, therefore, good reason for the controlled unfolding of the meaning of the symbol.

This concept of unfolding or unveiling was particularly developed by the 'Platonizing' school of Chartres in France, during the eleventh and twelfth centuries, most notably by Bernardus Silvestris in his commentary on Martianus Capella's *Marriage of Mercury and Philologia*.[2] In it, the commentator defines the practice of *integumentum*, which literally means 'cover' or 'wrapping' and usually referred to clothing. However, here we have the word used to refer specially to symbolic narratives and their hidden meanings. "Figurative discourse," says our Chartrain author, "is a mode of discourse which is called a veil. Figurative discourse is twofold, for we divide it into allegory and *integumentum*." He goes on to say, "Allegory pertains to Holy Scripture, but *integumentum* to philosophical scripture." Hence he explains that his commentary on Capella uses this latter method because Capella "is unveiling the deification of human nature," and "speaks like a prudent theologian, because all his utterances contain a hidden truth." The work contains instruction and this instruction has been put into figurative form.

Figuration can also be one of the values or qualities that the Divine Artificer uses to decorate or adorn the invisible first principles of the creation (the word *kosmos* for 'universe' means 'adornment'). Thus arithmetic and geometric figuration, with the resultant harmonic (musical) figurations, are the most essential tools that Plato posits the Divine Craftsman uses to adorn the 'likeness' of the perfect cosmos, which he is attempting to delineate in the psycho-cosmogony of the *Timaeus*.

There is not space here to develop all the interesting implications

---

1. The fragments of the philosopher Heraclitus contain many masterly examples of teaching by paradox. For instance, his fragment 48 is: "The bow is called life, but its work is death"—the Greek for both 'life' and 'bow' being the same, *bios*.

2. The commentary on Martianus Capella's *De Nuptiis Philologiae et Mercurii*, attributed to Bernardus Silvestris, edited by H.J. Westra, Pontifical Institute of Medieval Studies, Toronto, pp. 23-33.

of how 'four' is 'ten' and so on. So what we propose to do is to look at how Plato took care to reveal only so much of what are called by Aristotle the 'unwritten doctrines.'

When Plato proposed the portioning by number of the Same, Other and Being in their unified mixture (*Timaeus* 35b-c), he set up what has subsequently been called his Lambda. It is a portioning arranged into two 'arms,' each with three intervals.

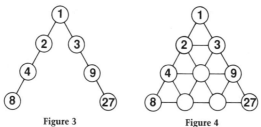

Figure 3   Figure 4

Figure 3. Plato's Lambda from the *Timaeus*. The first seven portions of the triadic mixture of Same, Other and Being corresponding to the seven planetary lights.
Figure 4. The missing positions in the Platonic Lambda.

Starting from one at the top, the generation from 1 to 2 and 3 gives the eventual seven stages. Here we see the principle of 'twice' and 'thrice' as well as the progression from 2 into a plane 4 and a cubic 8, while on the opposite arm is 3 with its plane 9 and cubic 27. Now we have seven positions representing two progressions, which leaves us with the impression that there could be three more 'points' or positions within the open triangle, so that if filled the model would become like the sacred Tetraktys of the Pythagoreans or the triangular 'four' representing the full decad. Even if Plato himself did not suggest the lambda form in the *Timaeus*, yet because the convention of triangular numbering and the image of the Tetraktys in four lines of dots were completely familiar to the Pythagoreans of the day, it would be inevitable that they would make the comparison. The idea of doing so is not new: the pattern we are about to look into was, in fact, published by the Pythagorean Nicomachus of Gerasa in the second century A.D.

Before proceeding further, we will do well to observe that we are allocating numbers to each of the 'dots' of the pure Tetraktys model (figure 1); we are accordingly already moving into symbolic representation. Each dot becomes representative of a position in the process of generation—from undifferentiated unity into 'twiceness' and 'thriceness' in the first dimension, 'fourness' and 'nineness' as their respective planar reflections, and 'eightness' and 'twenty-sevenness' as their projections into the ultimate third dimension or bodily world. We have two squared and cubed, and three squared and cubed, giving us a dyad of forms of generation passing through the three dimensions on each arm.

The challenge that follows the allocation of three more points within the triangle (figure 4) is to discover what numbers they should be, if they are not part of the existing progressions of 2 or 3. The solution becomes a matter of the logic of the symmetry or 'angles' that the progressions of 'times 2' and 'times 3' follow. If we start from the monad or one at the top and follow down the right-hand slope or angle, the fourfold progression is 1x3=3, x3=9, x3=27. If we now shift down from 1 to the position of 2 and follow a similar angle down through the pattern, we pass through the center point, which becomes 2x3=6, and arrive at the point on the base, which becomes 6x3=18. If we do the same, starting with the diagonal that moves down from 4, we have 4x3=12.

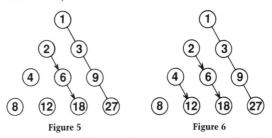

Figure 5   Figure 6

Figure 5. The generating angle of the 'times three' symmetry. Starting from 2 generating 6 and 18: 3x2=6, 3x6=18.

Figure 6. The second additional 'times three' diagonal angle from 4 creating 12 as 4x3=12.

Now, to check that this allocation is valid, we have the symmetrical diagonals following down the other way and multiplying by 2. Starting from 3 this time, we would get 3x2=6 and 6x2=12: the pattern agrees with the times-three symmetry. Finally, starting from 9, we have 9x2=18, which is the same result as on the times-three slope. The pattern is consistent and valid.

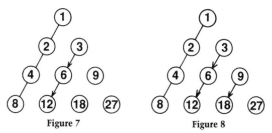

Figure 7   Figure 8

Figure 7. The generating angle of the 'times two' symmetry, from 3 generating 6 and 12: 2x3=6, 2x6=12.

Figure 8. The second 'times two' diagonal from 9 generating 18: 2x9=18.

Referring back to Aetius' statement of the Pythagorean position, that number has the Decad (or the Tetraktys, we might say) as its 'nature,' and that the numbers have 'symmetry' and produce 'harmony' within, then we now have a pattern with all those qualities simultaneously present—our numerically symbolic Tetraktys, developed from Plato's Timaean Lambda.

In summary, we might say that the point positions, one by one, represent the Decad; the sets of points represent the oneness, twoness, threeness and fourness of the constituent horizontal lines which we can call the first symmetry; the allocated number progressions represent 'states of being' of the refraction of one, we might say, and particularly of two and three respectively as they move from plane to cubic form and thereby provide a pattern that has within it the essential numerical harmonies. In particular, this Decad contains those numerical harmonies proposed by Plato for such a vital story as the generation of the 'world soul' in the *Timaeus*, as we shall see.

On the basis of simultaneous qualities interpenetrating and mutually present, we might take the point model as representative of the background archetypal 'isness' of the 'incomparable' ideal numbers—those complete at ten. In another sense, we could take the allocated soul-generating numbers to be representative of the numbers moving into bodiliness or cubic being and ready to facilitate the geometrical basis of materiality (*Timaeus* 36e, 53c-e). The geometrical basis of materiality consists of the tetrahedron or 'fourness' of fire or light, the octahedrality or 'sixness' of the gaseousness of air, the icosahedrality or 'twelveness' of the liquidity of water, and the cubic 'eightness' of the solid earthiness. These numbers are the points in space that define the solidity of the regular figures.

Each of the basic 'geometricals' can be generated out of a series of morphic points as three-dimensional reflections of the first monad or the 'original' singular spherical body—the sphere being the most perfect and most simple three-dimensional form, simultaneously representing the unique, unity and the unified.

However, to return to the significance of our number pattern.

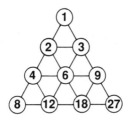

Figure 9. The Platonic Lambda filled out into the Pythagorean Tetraktys by the addition of 6, 12 and 18.

We learn from Plato that 'soul' embraces both the mean proportionals as well as the uniting principle of opposites (*Timaeus* 31c, 35a-b). We now can find out how the particular means, which Timaeus proposes the Divine Artificer uses to fill in the intervals between the primary numbers, can be found 'in the symmetries,' or in other words how the 'harmonies' can be read.

It is good to remember that Plato describes the cosmogony as 'a likely story,' indicating the objective laws that lie behind the ordering principles that we find in our cosmos, because this cosmos is only a 'likeness' of the ideal (*Timaeus* 29c). This cosmogony or creation story is a rhythmic separating and uniting of forces which are given 'provisional' names to enable us to even conceive of what is involved. First, there is the complementarity of Sameness and Otherness with their (proportional) uniting principle of Being. When the Divine Craftsman "made of them one out of three, straightaway He began to distribute this whole into so many portions..." (*Timaeus* 35b).

There follow the seven portions multiplying unity by two and three to get the sequence 1, 2, 3, 4, 9, 8, 27. Having made this division and related it to the sevenness of the planetary system, Plato goes on to describe the filling in of the intervals. This is done by placing two means between each of the powers of 2 and powers of 3. These are the arithmetic and harmonic means which, with the geometric mean, complete the triad of means. The means set up proportional unions between extremes and are therefore in themselves the epitome, in mathematical terms, of the mediating principle—in common with the definition of *psyche* ('soul') as mediating between the metaphysical (intelligible) domain and the physical (sensible) domain. The means themselves are set in a hierarchical tendency, as one might call it. The geometrical is the most heavenward (metaphysical), the harmonic the most central (psychic and anthropological), and the arithmetic the most earthward (physical).

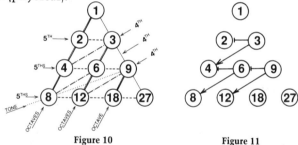

Figure 10   **Figure 11**

Figure 10. Tetraktys showing full display of musical ratios: the octave proportion of 2:1; the musical fifth proportion of 3:2; the musical fourth proportion of 4:3.; and the tone interval of 9:8.
Figure 11. The arithmetic proportion with the three arithmetic 'means' of 3, 6 and 9.

If we take these three means—the arithmetic, the harmonic and the geometric—we find that the legs or diagonals to the right or left are in geometric proportion (i.e. times 2 or times 3). The pattern in figure 11 above gives the symmetry of the arithmetical proportions. The mean is the middle (uniting) term between the two extremes; so we have 2, 3, 4, and 4, 6, 8, and 6, 9, 12, which are all examples of arithmetic proportion; and 3, 6 and 9 are the means or mid-terms. An arithmetic proportion, it should be noted, is one where the second term exceeds the first by the same amount as the third exceeds the second.

The harmonic proportion can be drawn as paths of symmetry within the pattern in the following way:

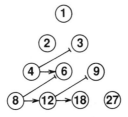

Figure 12. The harmonic proportions with the three harmonic means of 4, 8 and 12.

These new interior patterns give us the harmonic proportions of 3, 4, 6, and 6, 8, 12, and 9, 12, 18. The harmonic proportion is defined as the proportion where the mean exceeds one extreme and is exceeded by the other by the same fraction of the extremes (see *Timaeus* 36). If we take as an example 6, 8, 12, then eight exceeds six by one third of six (i.e. by two), and eight is exceeded by twelve by one third of 12 (i.e. by four).

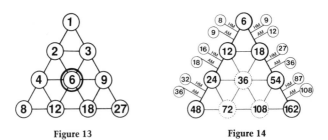

Figure 13   **Figure 14**

Figure 13. The central six as a key to the whole number intervals devised by Francesco Giorgi.
Figure 14. The whole-number arithmetic and harmonic intervals between each of the seven original numbers of Plato's Lambda as proposed by Francesco Giorgi. HM=Harmonic Mean; AM=Arithmetic Mean. Note that this results in there being the non-repeating sequence of 6, 8, 9, 12, 16, 18, 24, 27, 32, 36, 48, 54, 72, 87, 108 and 162: sixteen numbers of which the central number 36 occurs three times and is the square of 6 or 6 to the second power (6²).

The number six occupies the central point of our Tetraktys (figure 13). We can, as Francesco Giorgi did (inspired by Ficino's

commentary on the *Timaeus*),[3] multiply the peripheral original set
of seven numbers to arrive at figure 14. We have constructed a new
Tetraktys, based on unit 6. This results in the next insertions of
harmonic and arithmetic means, following the Timaean cosmogony as we did above, giving rise to a total series as follows (given by
F. Giorgi in his *De Harmonia Mundi Totius*, Venice, 1525): 6, 8, 9,
12, 16, 18, 24, 27, 32, 36, 48, 54, 81, 108, 162. The original seven are
underlined; the eight which are not underlined are harmonic or
arithmetic means between the sets above and display musical
ratios.

Francesco Giorgi gives another interesting veiled hint as to the
meaning of the three means in relation to the three realms or
domains. He calls the geometric mean the mean "par excellence,"
which we would propose refers to the heavenly or theological
realm. He calls the arithmetic mean "excess," which we propose
refers to the earthly or cosmological domain. Finally, he says of the
harmonic mean that it is "the harmony of the other two," which
in turn we would propose refers to the human, psychological or
anthropological domain. This links the three domains through the
metaphor of musical proportion, and with the pattern of the Sacred
Decad or Tetraktys.[4]

This is a deep subject that needs much more development than
current space permits. Our intention is mainly to indicate that the
'literature' of the Pythagorean tradition tends to be a stimulus or an
aid for the mind in its recall of the unwritten doctrines—or so it
would appear.

Finally, we are drawn to another idea that results from adding one
to each member of the first series:

3. See also pp. 83-5.

4. See the reference to Giorgi's work and its consequent influence on European architectural
theory in R. Wittkowa, *Architectural Principles in the Age of Humanism*, W.W. Norton, New
York, 1971, p. 112.

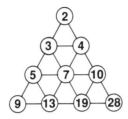

Figure 15. The 'new' Tetraktys starting with two or the 'indefinite dyad,' resulting in cosmic numbers or cycles.

2 The Sun and Moon, day and night.
3 The geocentric pattern of Mercury loops.
4 The four seasons or quarters of the year.
5 The geocentric pattern of Venus loops.
7 The cycle of the Moon's quarter or a week.
9 The trine conjunctions of Saturn and Jupiter over a 60-year period or a lifetime.
10 The Tetraktys.
13 The lunar months of the year.
19 The Metonic cycle of coincidence between Sun and Moon every 19th year.
28 The full cycle of the Moon.

This new set of numbers has an interesting cosmological quality; it includes numbers which were not represented in the previous set, and numbers that appear in the cosmic cycles. The apex takes up the generating role of the dyad or principle of multiplicity and thereby the created order. The first pair are the three and the four. Four completes the Decad in the sense we have explained, yet this first pair of 3 and 4 also represents threeness and fourness as 'spirit' and 'matter' or principle and expression—aspects of cosmic duality. Further, the cosmological seven of the planetary systems and one quarter of the lunar cycle (one week) are produced by 3+4, and seven takes up the central position of the 'new' Tetraktys. Five and ten, the 'quintessence' and the 'decad,' flank the seven. The nine, which is the last archetypal number before returning to the unity of the decad or ten, begins the row of the four lowest positions. Thirteen, which is the number of the occurrences of lunar cycles in a single year, as well as the number of closest-packed spheres around their nuclear sphere, is followed by the very special number nineteen, which is not only the magic number of years it takes for the sun and moon to be in the same relationship, but is also a sacred number for both the Holy Qu'ran and the Christian Gospels. Finally, twenty-eight is the full cycle of the moon's phases and is also the sum of the central number 7, because $1+2+3+4+5+6+7=28$. Taken arbitrarily, such facts can seem curiosities and usually do to those ignorant of arithmosophy, yet in the light of a wisdom teaching they demonstrate particular depths of symbolic value and meaning lying within the arrangement of numbers. These examples of interpretation are an indication that Plato put forward the Lambda pattern in the first instance as one of profound signification and yet left the inquiring mind to unfold the layers of meaning and the 'Pythagorean' source for themselves.

It has been said that written teachings are only ever partial (the Platonic *Seventh Letter* says as much), so we should expect the patterns given in the study of arithmosophy to appear simple and yet reveal more through sincere and genuine seeking. The truth, after all, is eventually one.

Both in the world and in man the decad is all.[5]

—KEITH CRITCHLOW

5. Philo of Alexandria, *Quaestiones et Solutiones in Genesim,* 4.110.

Introduction

The Theology of Arithmetic is a curious, but valuable work. It is preserved for us in the corpus of works of the eminent Neoplatonist Iamblichus, but it is almost certainly not the arithmological treatise he promised to write *(On Nicomachus' Introduction to Arithmetic,* 125.15 ff.): the author of our treatise is unknown.

This is, as far as I know, the first translation of the text out of its original Greek, let alone into a modern language. There are two main reasons for the neglect of the work. In the first place, Neoplatonism in general, and Neopythagoreanism in particular, are not popular studies in today's universities. Secondly, the text itself is undeniably scrappy.

The treatise is, in fact, a compilation and reads like a student's written-up notes. Whole sections are taken from the *Theology of Arithmetic* of the famous and influential mathematician and philosopher Nicomachus of Gerasa, and from the *On the Decad* of Iamblichus' teacher, Anatolius, Bishop of Laodicea. These two sources, which occupy the majority of our treatise, are linked by text whose origin is at best conjectural, but some of which could very well be lecture notes—perhaps even from lectures delivered by Iamblichus. At any rate, the treatise may tentatively be dated to the middle of the fourth century A.D.

The value of the treatise is threefold. First, from an academic point of view, given the author's eclecticism, he has preserved, or he reflects, work which would otherwise be lost to us: that of Nicomachus is especially important (Anatolius' book is independently preserved), but there is also, for instance, a long fragment of Speusippus, Plato's successor as head of the Academy in Athens.

The second, and related merit of the book is simply that we have little extended evidence of the vast tradition of arithmology (as distinct from the hard science of mathematics) among the Greeks; *The Theology of Arithmetic* is a welcome, if sometimes obscure, addition to the slender corpus of such texts.

The third chief merit of the treatise is harder to explain. Pythagoras of Samos lived towards the end of the sixth century B.C. Our

knowledge of his work and that of his successors is usually
tantalizingly scanty, but enough is preserved to be sure that, while
in exoteric areas such as mathematics there was considerable
development, the esoteric and religious side of their work remained
firmly based on the same principles and fully deserves to be called
the Pythagorean tradition, which lasted for at least a thousand
years. At any rate, to anyone familiar with the fragments of
Pythagoreanism and Neopythagoreanism, it is immediately clear
that a great deal of what *The Theology of Arithmetic* says could
equally well have been said, and in many cases was, by a Pythagorean of the fifth or fourth centuries B.C.

I shall say a little more about this Pythagorean arithmological
tradition shortly; here I need only say the following about it. Like
Kabbalists, they recognized ten principles of all things. These ten
principles are equated with, or described as, the first cycle of ten
numbers. Thus our treatise simply takes each of the numbers from
one to ten, and spends a few pages describing its qualities and giving
reasons for those qualities. These qualities are primarily mathematical, and then by extension allegorical. So, for instance, the
number one is present in all numbers and makes them what they
are. This is a straightforward mathematical proposition; an extension is to call the number one Intellect, Artificer, Prometheus.

This approach has often been called superstitious mumbo-
jumbo, but it is really only a different theological approach to ones
with which we are more familiar. Mathematics is the most abstract
language known to mankind;[1] to base a theology upon it is to
attempt to describe the abstract laws, as distinct from their appli-
cations, which govern God's universe. The outstanding nature of
The Theology of Arithmetic, and its third chief merit, is that at one
level it is unexceptionable, and fairly simple, Greek mathematics
(since the complexity of mathematics lies in proving theorems, not
merely in using the terminology, axioms or conclusions)—but the
simplest mathematical statement is simultaneously imbued with
religious import. The text makes it clear that for the Pythagoreans

---

1. As my friend Steve Lee (to whom this book is dedicated) once put it: "How could you
communicate with an intelligent, but totally alien species, except by means of number?"

mathematics was more than a science: God manifests in the mathematical laws which govern everything, and the understanding of those laws, and even simply doing mathematics, could bring one closer to God.

In the Western world, arithmology is inevitably associated with the name of Pythagoras and his followers. It should not, however, be forgotten that long after the demise of the Pythagorean schools number mysticism was still flourishing among Jewish and Christian mystics. The study and use of gematria by Jewish Kabbalists is relatively well known; more often forgotten is the fact that even such seminal Christian writers as John of Ruysbroeck (1293-1381) were perfectly prepared to see numbers as authoritative symbols and paradigms of divine principles.[2]

Among the Greeks, arithmology enjoyed a long history, as has already been remarked. It was practiced and studied concurrently with the science of mathematics, and by the same practitioners. As far as we can tell, no sooner had the Greeks been prompted (probably by contact with the Middle East) to elevate mathematics out of the market-place and into a pure science, than they also began to perceive philosophical and religious connotations to what they were doing. It is not too misleading a generalization to say that the Greek philosophers were impressed by the apparent orderliness of the universe and that this was for them the chief argument for some Intelligence being behind the universe. The Pythagoreans simply attributed this orderliness to the presence of number: numbers contain and manifest the laws of God's universe. Since all numbers after ten are repetitions of the first cycle, the first decad of numbers alone manifest these principles.

In passing, it should be noted that the idea that the laws which govern the universe are numerical is not in itself at all silly. It is not just that we are happy with formulae such as $E=mc^2$: these are perhaps different in that they are supported by scientific proof. More significant is the fact that we are still happy to accept more

---

2. I am thinking in particular of his *A Commentary on the Tabernacle of the Covenant*; but this is only now being translated, under the aegis of the Ruusbroecgenootschap of Holland.

mysterious mathematical phenomena, like the Fibonacci series of
natural growth, or Bode's law of the distances between planets, and
a host of other series and constants. Do we, I wonder, have the right
to praise these as scientific, but condemn the Pythagoreans as
irrational?

It should also be noted that while the Pythagorean attempt to
give meaning to peculiar properties of number is unfashionably
mystical, such peculiar properties have not been explained or
explained away by modern mathematicians. They exist, and one
either ignores them and gets on with doing mathematics, or gives
them significance, which is what arithmologists do.

The beginnings of arithmology among Pythagoras and his
immediate successors are unknown. Both mathematics and its
mystical counterpart belonged at that time to the oral tradition. By
the end of the fifth century B.C., however, it is certain that
Philolaus of Croton was writing arithmology down; perhaps his
great fame depends upon his having been the first to do so system-
atically. A number of fragments of his work are extant, but the
genuineness of many of them is disputed. Enough remains, however, to afford glimpses into an arithmology which is not vastly
different, in content or in quality, to what we find in our treatise.

The two great names from the beginning of the fourth century
B.C. are Archytas of Tarentum and, of course, Plato. It is certain
that Archytas made advances in the science of mathematics; but
my opinion is that he left arithmology pretty much as he found it,
though he certainly wrote on the subject. As for Plato, whose
enthusiasm for mathematics (and arithmology, especially in *Timaeus,* certain parts of *Republic, Epinomis* and in his unwritten
doctrines as reported by Aristotle and others) cannot be overesti-
mated, it is an insoluble argument whether he borrowed from a
tradition or was innovative in the field. Those who do not wish his
greatness to be tarnished by the suggestion of plagiarism should
remember that in the ancient world the borrowing of material was
not theft but a sign of respect. It is likely that he both drew on and

developed the tradition.[3] Plato's Academy certainly nurtured both mathematics and arithmology, as we can tell from the titles of lost books written by Speusippus and Xenocrates, his successors as heads of the Academy, and by the presence in the Academy of the eminent mathematician Eudoxus of Cnidos and others.

In the centuries following Plato, the science of mathematics was developed in technical works such as those of Euclid, Archimedes, Heron and Pappus, but the history of arithmology becomes obscure. It is not until the first century A.D. that we again start to have extant texts. The fragmentary evidence from the intervening centuries allows us to be sure that arithmological tenets were used in various commentaries on Plato's dialogues (especially *Timaeus*, of course); but the mainstream of progress can only be conjectured. That there was progress is clear: in the first place, arithmologists would have borrowed useful developments of mathematics, as corroborative evidence for some property of some number within the decad, or more generally as confirmation of the importance of number in the universe; in the second place, the extant texts of later centuries assign more properties to numbers within the decad than we can safely say were assigned in earlier centuries, which suggests that the intervening period was when these properties began to be assigned; and thirdly, as philosophical fashions came and went, arithmology absorbed the language and some of the doctrines of Platonism, Aristotelianism and Stoicism. More importantly, the later extant texts often show a high degree of unanimity of thought and even of language. This suggests that there was some common seminal writer, whose name is unknown to us (it used to be thought to be the polymath Posidonius (*c.* 135-*c.* 50 B.C.), but who can be dated to the second century B.C.[4]

3. To the extent that a tradition can be said to be developed; it is more accurate to say that it can be clothed in different forms.

4. See F.E. Robbins, "The Tradition of Greek Arithmology," *Classical Philology* 1921, pp. 97-123.

This unknown teacher seems to have given a new impetus to Pythagoreanism. The name of Pythagoras was no doubt never far from the lips of all the arithmologists of these centuries; but in the first century B.C., in Rome and Alexandria, thinkers again began to claim direct descent from the master, and we nowadays call them the Neopythagoreans. Many of these philosophers, such as Publius Nigidius Figulus (first century B.C.), Apollonius of Tyana (first century A.D.) and Numenius of Apamea (second century A.D.) are little more than names to us now, though the work of others like Theon of Smyrna and Nicomachus of Gerasa, who were contemporaries at the beginning of the second century A.D., is better preserved. It is unlikely that we are dealing with a unified school of thought, but nevertheless the influence of this Pythagorean revival was great. It was especially strong over the Neoplatonists, but the early Neopythagoreans also paved the way for Greek arithmology to enter the Jewish tradition via the works of Philo of Alexandria, and the Christian tradition via the works of Clement of Alexandria.

Now, this potted history of Greek arithmology is meant only to illuminate our treatise by putting it in context. What I have called the 'lecture-note' style of the book already warns us, and the context of the vast arithmological tradition confirms, that the best approach would be to regard nothing in the book as original to the anonymous compiler, and to remember that far more ancient arithmology is lost than is extant.

It is not just that our author liberally quotes from Nicomachus and Anatolius, nor that much of what our treatise says can be found here and there in other books. It is also that, apart from one or two more extended and discursive passages (such as the discussion of the relation between the pentad and justice), one constantly gets the impression that we are being shown the tip of an iceberg—that far more arithmological speculation was available than we know from treatises such as *The Theology of Arithmetic* or occasional remarks in other philosophers.

As Keith Critchlow's foreword suggests, the most convincing way to demonstrate this is to practice a little arithmology ourselves. In the last pages of the book, we find Anatolius associating the numbers 36 and 55 in various way. However, he omits one context in which these numbers may be related, and this context is so obvious that it must have been known to the Greeks. It would have been obvious because it stems from Plato, whose authority was revered.[5]

In *Timaeus*, Plato declared that the primary sequence of numbers by which the universe gains life is 1, 2, 3, 4, 9, 8, 27; these numbers are displayed on a lambda diagram as follows:

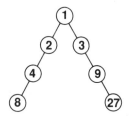

A natural addition to this diagram, which completes it in the sense that it becomes a tetraktys (see Keith Critchlow's foreword), is to insert the geometrical means:

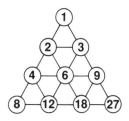

Three things immediately become clear: that the three means we have inserted add up to 36; that the three apexes of the triangle add up to 36; and that the diagram now contains all the factors of 36, which, as our author says, add up to 55. (A fourth point, that the separate double and triple series down the arms of the lambda add

5. For what follows, I am indebted to Rod Thorn.

up to 55, is mentioned by Anatolius.)

This slight example of such speculation is deliberately intended to encourage others to do the same, as well as to support my contention that we are faced in *The Theology of Arithmetic* with the tip of an iceberg. An academic cannot acknowledge such speculation as evidence: his or her discipline is necessarily and rightly rooted in the available textual evidence—otherwise it fails to be the valuable mental discipline that it is. But I think that such speculation, provided it is not too extravagant, can afford personal insights, at any rate, into what the Pythagorean tradition was concerned with.

The Greek text I have used in preparing this translation is that of V. de Falco (Teubner series, Leipzig, 1922; additional notes by U. Klein, 1975.) De Falco's text is the most recent edition, and this was only the second time that the Greek had been critically edited: the first such edition was by F. Ast (Leipzig, 1817). Nevertheless, because of the lecture-note style of the text, and because of its inherent difficulties, over the centuries the Greek has become corrupted in many places: much more work even than that of Ast, de Falco and others remains to be done. Possibly some passages will never be recoverable: at any rate, I have often felt constrained to differ from de Falco's extremely conservative text (those who are interested are referred to my article in *Classical Quarterly* 1988). For those who want to compare the translation with the Greek text, I have inserted de Falco's page numbers in square brackets throughout the translation for ease of cross-reference.

A convention I have used in the translation needs mentioning. Our author often indicates by various Greek grammatical devices when he is changing from one source (say, Nicomachus) to another (say, Anatolius, or even a different bit of Nicomachus). I have indicated such changes by leaving an extra line space in the text (a single centered asterisk is used when such a break coincides with the end of a page). Sometimes he jumps alarmingly from one source to another: on p. 39, for instance, he attributes the content of one sentence to Anatolius, then skips to an unattributed doctrine (which is probably from Nicomachus), only to revert, without attribution, to Anatolius a couple of lines later. For those who read German, there is an excellent account of this aspect of our treatise by H. Oppermann, in the course of his review of de Falco's edition in *Gnomon* 1929, pp. 545-58.

It was tempting to clutter up the pages with many footnotes, but I have tried to keep these to a minimum. I have footnoted only those passages where I felt that the meaning might not be clear even on a second or third reading. There is a high degree of subjectivity about this, of course: what I think readers will find difficult to understand is not necessarily what any reader will find difficult to understand. It may be assumed, anyway, that those passages without footnotes are ones where I felt that a little thought could reveal the meaning. However, there are one or two sentences which lack footnotes not for this reason, but because I completely fail to understand them!

I owe a particular debt of gratitude to Keith Critchlow and Kairos for being easily persuaded that it would be worthwhile to translate and publish *The Theology of Arithmetic*. Several others have helped me to understand one or more passages of the treatise, and I would like to acknowledge such assistance from the following people: Professor John Dillon, Dr. Vivian Nutton, Dr. David Sedley, Rod Thorn, Annie McCombe, Peter Thomas and Keith Munnings. It goes without saying that none of them are responsible for any remaining defects in quality and tone of my translation or commentary.

—ROBIN WATERFIELD

ΤΑ ΘΕΟΛΟΓΟΥΜΕΝΑ ΤΗΣ ΑΡΙΘΜΗΤΙΚΗΣ

On the Monad

[1] The monad is the non-spatial source of number. It is called 'monad' because of its stability,[1] since it preserves the specific identity of any number with which it is conjoined. For instance, 3x1=3, 4x1=4: see how the approach of the monad to these numbers preserved the same identity and did not produce a different number.

Everything has been organized by the monad, because it contains everything potentially: for even if they are not yet actual, nevertheless the monad holds seminally the principles which are within all numbers, including those which are within the dyad. For the monad is even and odd and even-odd;[2] linear and plane and solid (cubical and spherical and in the form of pyramids from those with four angles to those with an indefinite number of angles); perfect and over-perfect and defective; proportionate and harmonic; prime and incomposite, and secondary; diagonal and side; and it is the source of every relation, whether one of equality or inequality, as has been proved in the *Introduction*.[3] Moreover, it is demonstrably both point and angle (with all forms of angle), and beginning, middle and end of all things, since, if you [2] decrease it, it limits the infinite dissection of what is continuous, and if you increase it, it defines the increase as being the same as the dividends (and this is due to the disposition of divine, not human, nature.)[4]

1. The author follows a traditional etymology of *monas* and derives it from *menein* (to be stable).

2. For these and other terms, see the Glossary. The monad is called both even and odd because if it is added to an even number, the result is odd, while if it is added to an odd number, the result is even. It was therefore held to have the properties of both evenness and oddness.

3. The reference is probably to Nicomachus, *Introduction to Arithmetic*, I.23.4-17 and II.2.1-2. Assuming that the monad is the source of equality because the first manifestation of equality is 1=1, then those passages are relevant, because they argue that all forms of inequality (see p. 79, n. 14) are derivable from equality and reducible back to it.

4. The text of this sentence is extremely difficult and there may be a lacuna before 'since,' but it seems to mean, first, if you take 1/n, then however many parts 1 is divided into, each part is

At any rate (as was demonstrated at the beginning of the *Arithmetic* in the lambda-shaped diagram),[5] each of the parts within the monad correspond to and offset the integers. Hence, just as if x is double y, then x^2 is four times y^2, and x^3 is eight times y^3, and if x is triple y, then x^2 is nine times y^2, and x^3 is twenty-seven time y^3, in the orderly arrangement of all numbers; so also in the orderly arrangement of parts, if x is half y, then x^2 is one quarter y^2, and x^3 is one eighth y^3, and if x is one third y, then x^2 is one ninth y^2, and x^3 is one twenty-seventh y^3.

Every compound of plurality or every subdivision is given form by the monad; for the decad is one and the chiliad is one, and again one tenth is one and one thousandth is one, and so on for all the subdivisions *ad infinitum*.

In each of these cases there is the same monad in terms of form, yet different monads in respect of quantity, because it produces itself out of itself, as well as producing them, just as if it were the principle of the universe and the nature of things; and because it maintains everything and forbids whatever it is present in to change, it alone of all numbers resembles the Providence which preserves everything, and is most particularly suited both to reflect the principle of God and to be likened to him, in so far as it is closest to him.

It is in fact the form of forms, since it is creation thanks to its creativity and intellect thanks to its intelligence; this is adequately demonstrated in the [3] mutual opposition of oblongs and squares.[6]

still a monad in its own right; second, if you take n/1, then n is still 1+1+1 ... n.

5. The familiarity of the reference makes it seem as though it is again to Nicomachus' *Introduction* (see p. 35, n. 3), but there is no lambda-shaped diagram near the start of that. However, in his commentary on Nicomachus' book, Iamblichus derives from it a lambda diagram which demonstrates the 'natural contrariety' of integers and fractions. So the reference *is* to Nicomachus, but as commented on by Iamblichus (14.3 ff.). The application of Iamblichus' diagram which is relevant to our text is as follows:

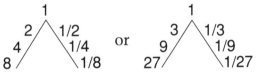

6. Nicomachus, *Introduction to Arithmetic* II.19, argues that the whole universe is skilfully

*

Nicomachus says that God coincides with the monad, since he is seminally everything which exists, just as the monad is in the case of number; and there are encompassed in it in potential things which, when actual, seem to be extremely opposed (in all the ways in which things may, generally speaking, be opposed), just as it is seen, throughout the *Introduction to Arithmetic*, to be capable, thanks to its ineffable nature, of becoming all classes of things, and to have encompassed the beginning, middle and end of all things (whether we understand them to be composed by continuity or by juxtaposition),[7] because the monad is the beginning, middle and end of quantity, of size and moreover of every quality.

Just as without the monad there is in general no composition of anything, so also without it there is no knowledge of anything whatsoever, since it is a pure light, most authoritative over everything in general, and it is sun-like and ruling, so that in each of these respects it resembles God, and especially because it has the power of making things cohere and combine, even when they are composed of many ingredients and are very different from one another, just as he made this universe harmonious and unified out of things which are likewise opposed.

Furthermore, the monad produces itself and is produced from itself, since it is self-sufficient and has no power set over it and is everlasting; and it is evidently the cause of permanence, just as God is thought to be in the case of actual physical things, and to be the preserver and maintainer of natures.

So they[8] say that the monad is not only God, but also 'intellect' [4] and 'androgyne.' It is called 'intellect' because of that aspect of God which is the most authoritative both in the creation of the universe and in general in all skill and reason: even if this aspect of God were not to manifest itself as a whole in particular matters, yet in respect of its activity it is Intellect, since in respect of its knowledge it is sameness and unvarying. Just so, the monad, which

contrived by harmonizing the opposition of the sequences of squares and oblong numbers.

7. See e.g. pp. 55, 60, n. 13: all things are either continuous and have size, or are juxtaposed and have quantity.

8. Any unattributed 'they' in this treatise means 'the Pythagoreans.'

even if differentiated in the different kinds of thing has conceptually encompassed everything within itself, is as it were a creative
principle and resembles God, and does not alter from its own
principle, and forbids anything else to alter, but is truly unchanging
and is the Fate Atropos.[9]

That is why it is called 'artificer' and 'modeler,' since in its
processions and recessions it takes thought for the mathematical
natures, from which arise instances of corporeality, of propagation
of creatures and of the composition of the universe. Hence they call
it 'Prometheus,' the artificer of life, because, uniquely, it in no way
outruns or departs from its own principle,[10] nor allows anything
else to do so, since it shares out its own properties. For however far
it is extended, or however many extensions it causes, it still
prohibits outrunning and changing the fundamental principle of
itself and of those extensions.

So, in short, they consider it to be the seed of all, and both male
and female at once—not only because they think that what is odd
is male in so far as it is [5] hard to divide and what is even is female
in so far as it is easy to separate, and it alone is both even and odd,
but also because it is taken to be father and mother, since it
contains the principles of both matter and form, of craftsman and
what is crafted; that is to say, when it is divided, it gives rise to the
dyad. (For it is easier for a craftsman to procure matter for himself
than for the reverse to happen—for matter to procure a craftsman.)[11] And the seed which is, as far as its own nature is concerned,
capable of producing both females and males, when scattered not
only produces the nature of both without distinction, but also does
so during pregnancy up to a certain point; but when it begins to be
formed into a foetus and to grow, it then admits distinction and
variation one way or the other, as it passes from potentiality to
actuality.[12]

9. One of three Fates: her name means 'not to be turned aside.'

10. The etymology of Prometheus is here derived from the Greek for 'not outrunning.'

11. Here the argument is that the monad take precedence over the dyad (see also p. 42), but
on p. 46 there is an argument that they co-exist. Both passages are probably from Nicomachus,
so they should be resolved into the idea that the monad is the most important of the primary
and co-existent pair of sources, the monad and the dyad, or sameness and difference.

12. The relevant tenets of Greek embryology are that the father gives form, the mother matter;

If the potential of every number is in the monad, then the monad would be intelligible number in the strict sense, since it is not yet manifesting anything actual, but everything is conceptually together in it.

There is a certain plausibility in their also calling it 'matter' and even 'receptacle of all,' since it is productive even of the dyad (which is matter, strictly speaking) and since it is capable of containing all principles; for it is in fact productive and disposed to share itself with everything.

Likewise, they call it 'Chaos,' which is Hesiod's first generator,[13] because Chaos gives rise to everything else, as the monad does. It is also thought to be both 'mixture' and 'blending,' 'obscurity' and 'darkness,' thanks to the lack of articulation and distinction of everything which ensues from it.

Anatolius says that it is called 'matrix' and 'matter,' on the grounds that without it there is no number.

The mark which signifies the monad is a symbol of the source of all things.[14] [6] And it reveals its kinship with the sun in the summation of its name: for the word 'monad' when added up yields 361, which are the degrees of the zodiacal circle.[15]

The Pythagoreans called the monad 'intellect' because they thought that intellect was akin to the One; for among the virtues, they likened the monad to moral wisdom; for what is correct is one. And they called it 'being,' 'cause of truth,' 'simple,' 'paradigm,' 'order,' 'concord,' 'what is equal among greater and lesser,' 'the mean between intensity and slackness,' 'moderation in plurality,' 'the instant now in time,' and moreover they called it 'ship,'

and that differentiation of gender does not occur for the first few days of pregnancy (cf. pp. 83-4, 93-4).

13. Hesiod, Theogony 116.

14. Presumably α (alpha) is the 'mark which signifies the monad' (see next note). It starts the word arche (source).

15. The letters of the Greek alphabet also served as numerical symbols: hence a system of gematria was obvious. The Greek monas is 40+70+50+1+200. Presumably 361, rather than 360, is given as the number of degrees because the first one is counted twice, to indicate a complete

'chariot,' 'friend,' 'life,' 'happiness.'

Furthermore, they say that in the middle of the four elements there lies a certain monadic fiery cube, whose central position they say Homer was aware of when he said: "As far beneath as is Hades, so far above the Earth are the heavens."[16] In this context, it looks as though the disciples of Empedocles and Parmenides and just about the majority of the sages of old followed the Pythagoreans and declared that the principle of the monad is situated in the middle in the manner of the Hearth, and keeps its location because of being equilibrated; and Euripides too, who was a disciple of Anaxagoras, mentions the Earth as follows: "Those among mortals who are wise consider you to be the Hearth."[17]

Moreover, [7] the Pythagoreans say that the right-angled triangle too was formed by Pythagoras when he regarded the numbers in the triangle monad by monad.[18]

The Pythagoreans link matter closely with the dyad. For matter is the source of differentiation in Nature, while the dyad is the source of differentiation in number; and just as matter is indefinite and formless, so also, uniquely among all numbers, the dyad is incapable of receiving form. Not least for the following reason also the dyad can be called indefinite: shape is encompassed in actuality by means of at least and in the first instance three angles or lines, while the monad is in potential.[19]

Calling the monad 'Proteus,' as they do, is not implausible, since he was the demigod in Egypt who could assume any form and contained the properties of everything, as the monad is the factor of each number.

circle.
  16. *Iliad* 8.16. See p. 106, n. 15, for the four-element model of the universe.
  17. Euripides, fragment 938 (Nauck²).
  18. See p. 82, perhaps.
  19. I am fairly sure that this paragraph is out of place and belongs somewhere in the section on the dyad.

On the Dyad

From Anatolius

Adding dyad to dyad is equivalent to multiplying them: adding them and multiplying them have the same result, and yet in all other cases multiplication is greater than addition.

Among the virtues, they liken it to courage: for it has already advanced into action. Hence too they used to call it 'daring' [8] and 'impulse.'

They also gave it the title of 'opinion,' because truth and falsity lie in opinion. And they called it 'movement,' 'generation,' 'change,' 'division,' 'length,' 'multiplication,' 'addition,' 'kinship,' 'relativity,' 'the ratio in proportionality.' For the relation of two numbers is of every conceivable form.

So the dyad alone remains without form and without the limitation of being contained by three terms and proportionality, and is opposed and contrary to the monad beyond all other numerical terms (as matter is contrary to God, or body to incorporeality), and is as it were the source and foundation of the diversity of numbers, and hence resembles matter; and the dyad is all but contrasted to the nature of God in the sense that it is considered to be the cause of things changing and altering, while God is the cause of sameness and unchanging stability.

So each thing and the universe as a whole is one as regards the natural and constitutive monad in it, but again each is divisible, in so far as it necessarily partakes of the material dyad as well. Hence the first conjunction of monad and dyad results in the first finite plurality, the element of things, which would be a triangle of quantities and numbers, both corporeal and incorporeal. For just as the sap of the fig tree congeals liquid milk because of its active and productive property, so when the unificatory power of the monad

41

approaches the dyad, which is [9] the fount of flowing and liquidity, it instills limit and gives form (i.e. number) to the triad. For the triad is the source in actuality of number, which is by definition a system a monads. But in a sense the dyad is a monad on account of being like a source.

The dyad gets its name from passing through or asunder;[1] for the dyad is the first to have separated itself from the monad, whence also it is called 'daring.' For when the monad manifests unification, the dyad steals in and manifests separation.

It rules over the category of relativity too, either by virtue of its ratio as regards the monad, which is double, or by virtue of its ratio as regards the next number after it, which is sesquialter; and these ratios are the roots of the ratios which extend infinitely in either direction, with the consequence that the dyad is also in this respect the source of multiplication and division.

The dyad is also an element in the composition of all things, an element which is opposed to the monad, and for this reason the dyad is perpetually subordinate to the monad, as matter is to form.
Hence, since form is capable of conceiving being and eternal existence, but matter is capable of conceiving the opposites to these,[2] the monad is the cause of things which are altogether

1. *Duas* (dyad) is here linked with *dia* (through or asunder).
2. For help with what follows, see Glossary under *Gnomon* for the relation between squares and the sequence of odd numbers, and between oblongs and the sequence of even numbers. The race-track image which follows should be considered like this: in the case of squares, the race-course is formed of successive numbers from 1 to n, which is the length of the side of the square in question, and is the turning-point; the return journey goes back through (n-1), (n-2) . . . to 1 again. Thus a square whose sides are 4 in length has an outward journey of 1+2+3, a turning-post of 4, and a return journey of 3+2+1; the sum total is 16, the area of the square.
However, in the case of oblongs (or, strictly heteromecics: see Glossary under *Oblong*), things are different. Heteromecics start from 2, so the outward journey of a heteromecic whose sides are 5 and 4 in length is 2+3+4, the turning post is 5, and the return journey is 3+2+1. The total (20) is again the area of the heteromecic in question, but the journeying of heteromecics does not have the same finishing-point as starting-point, as squares do. Heteromecics start with 2, but end with 1. This, I suppose, is why at the end of the paragraph they are said to 'admit destruction,' because destruction is severance from one's cause: the cause of heteromecics is 2, but they do not return there.

similar and identical and stable (i.e. of squares), not only because
the sequence of odd numbers, which are formed by the monad,
encompass it like gnomons and produce squares by cumulative
arithmetical progression (that is, they result in the infinite sequence of squares), but also because each side, like the turning-
point in a race from the monad as starting-point and to the monad
as winning-post, contains the square itself, as it adds its outward
journey to return journey. On the other hand, [10] the dyad is the
cause of things which are altogether dissimilar (i.e. of oblongs), not
only because the kinds of things which are formed by it are the even
numbers, which encompass it like gnomons, and which are produced in cumulative progression, but also because—to take the
same image of turning-point, finishing-post and starting-point—
whereas the monad, as the cause of sameness and stability in
general, seems also to give rise to generation, the dyad seems to
admit destruction and to admit return journeys which are different
from its outward journeys, so that it is a material substance and
capable of admitting every kind of destruction.

The dyad would be the mid-point between plurality, which is
regarded as falling under the triad, and that which is opposed to
plurality, which falls under the monad. Hence it simultaneously
has the properties of both. It is the property of 1, as source, to make
something more by addition than by the blending power of multiplication[3] (and that is why 1+1 is more than 1x1), and it is the
property of plurality, on the other hand, as product, to do the
opposite: for it makes something more by multiplication than by
addition. For plurality is no longer like a source, but each number
is generated one out of another and by blending[4] (and that is why
3x3 is more than 3+3). And while the monad and the triad have
opposite properties, the dyad is, as it were, the mean, and will admit
the properties of both at once, as it occupies the mid-point between

3. The source of something is already in it; hence if you blend (multiply) something with its
source, no increase occurs.
4. The Pythagorean tradition was actually ambivalent about whether the sequence of
numbers was generated simply by addition, or whether multiplication was the cause. Traces of
this ambivalence will recur in our treatise.

each. And we say that the mean between what is greater and what is smaller is what is equal. Therefore equality lies in this number alone. Therefore the product of its multiplication will be equal to the sum of its addition: [11] for 2+2=2x2. Hence they used to call it 'equal.'

That it also causes everything which directly relates to it to have the same property of being equal is clear not only (and this is why it is the first to express equality in a plane and solid fashion— equality of length and breadth in the plane number 4, and in the solid number eight equality of depth and height as well) in its very divisibility into two monads which are equal to each other, but also in the number which is said to be 'evolved' from it (that is, 16, which is 2x2x2x2), which is a plane number of the so-called 'color' on base 2: for 16 is 4x4.[5] And this number is obviously in a sense a sort of mean between greater and lesser in the same way that the dyad is. For the squares before it have perimeters which are greater than their surface areas, while the squares after it, on the other hand, have perimeters which are less than their surface areas, but this square alone has perimeter equal to surface area.[6] This is apparently why Plato in *Theaetetus* went up to 16, but stopped 'for some reason' at the square whose area is 17 feet, when he was faced with the manifestation of the specific property of 16 and the appearance of a certain shared equality.[7]

With regard to what, therefore, did the ancients call the dyad 'inequality' and 'deficiency and excess'? Because it is taken to be matter, and if it is the first in which distance and the notion of linearity are visible, then here is the source of difference and of inequality; and besides because, to assess it in terms of what precedes it, it is more, while to assess the tetrad [12] in terms of what precede *it* , the tetrad is less, and the triad is in the middle of

5. 'Color' is a traditional Pythagorean term for surface area. Thus 16 is a 'plane number' (i.e. square) of the 'color on base 2' (i.e. 2 squared, or 4).

6. A square whose area is 16 has four sides each 4 in length: the sum of the sides is also 16. Smaller squares have areas less than the sum of their sides; larger squares have areas greater than the sum of their sides.

7. That is, the equality shared by the area and the sum of the sides (see previous note). See Plato, *Theaetetus* 147d.

these two. So by this alternative approach it will follow, contrary to what we found earlier,[8] that the triad, rather than what precedes it, contains the principle of equality. For 2 is greater than what precedes it (I mean 1) in the first manifestation of the relation of being greater, and 4 is less than 3+2+1 in the first manifestation of the relation of being less, and 3 is equal to 2+1 and falls under the relation of equality, which is indivisible, with the consequence that the linear number 2 is consonant with what is more, but when raised to a plane number it is consonant with what is less.

It is also called 'deficiency and excess' and 'matter' (for which, in fact, another term is the 'indefinite dyad') because it is in itself devoid of shape and form and any limitation, but is capable of being limited and made definite by reason and skill.

The dyad is clearly formless, because the infinite sequence of polygons arise in actuality from triangularity and the triad, while as a result of the monad everything is together in potential, and no rectilinear figure consists of two straight lines or two angles. So what is indefinite and formless falls under the dyad alone.

It also turns out to be 'infinity,' since it is difference, and difference starts from its being set against 1 and extends to infinity. And it can be described as productive of infinity, since the first manifestation of length is in the dyad, based on the monad as a point, and length is both infinitely divisible and infinitely extensible. Moreover, the nature of inequality proceeds in an infinite sequence whose source is the dyad [13] in opposition to the monad. For the primary distinction between them is that one is greater, the other smaller.

The dyad is not number, nor even, because it is not actual; at any rate, every even number is divisible into both equal and unequal parts, but the dyad alone cannot be divided into unequal parts; and also, when it is divided into equal parts, it is completely unclear to which class its parts belong, as it is like a source.[9]

*

8. See pp. 43-4.

9. It is unclear whether its parts are odd or even, since the monad is both odd and even.

The dyad, they say, is also called 'Erato'; for having attracted through love the advance of the monad as form, it generates the rest of the results, starting with the triad and tetrad.[10]

Apart from recklessness itself, they think that, because it is the very first to have endured separation, it deserves to be called 'anguish,' 'endurance' and 'hardship.'[11]

From division into two, they call it 'justice' (as it were 'dichotomy'),[12] and they call it 'Isis,' not only because the product of its multiplication is equal to the sum of its addition, as we said,[13] but also because it alone does not admit division into unequal parts.

And they call it 'Nature,' since it is movement towards being and, as it were, a sort of coming-to-be and extension from a seed principle;[14] and this is why it is so called, because movement from one thing to another is in the likeness of the dyad.

Some people, however, misled by numbers which are already countable and secondary, instruct us to regard the dyad as a system of two monads, with the result that if dissolved it reverts to these same monads. But if the dyad is a system of monads,[15] then [14] the monads are generated earlier; and if the monad is half the dyad, then the existence of the dyad is necessarily prior. If their mutual relations are to be preserved for them, they necessarily co-exist, because double is double what is half, and half is half what is double, and they are neither prior nor posterior, because they generate and are generated by each other, destroy and are destroyed by each other.

They also name it 'Diometor', the mother of Zeus (they said that the monad was 'Zeus'), and 'Rhea', after its flux and extension,[16] which are the properties both of the dyad and of Nature, which is

10. Erato is one of the Muses; her name is cognate with the Greek for 'love.'

11. *Duas* (dyad) is here linked with *due* (anguish).

12. The Greek for 'justice' is *dike*, 'dichotomy' *diche.*

13. Here Nicomachus links Isis with *ison* (equal); then pp. 43-4 are referred to (see also p. 41, from Anatolius).

14. The word for 'Nature' is cognate with 'growth'; the 'seed principle' is the monad (see e.g. pp. 35, 50).

15. Which is the definition of *actual* number (see p. 51).

16. The name Rhea (the mother of the Gods and of Nature) is similar to the Greek for 'flux.'

in all respects coming into being. And they say that the name 'dyad' is suited to the moon, both because it admits of more settings than any of the other planets,[17] and because the moon is halved or divided into two: for it is said to be cut into half or into two.

17. Here *duas* (dyad) is linked with *duseis* (settings).

On the Triad

The triad has a special beauty and fairness beyond all numbers, primarily because it is the very first to make actual the potentialities of the monad—oddness, perfection, proportionality, unification, limit. For 3 is the first number to be actually odd, since in conformity with its descriptions it is 'more than equal' and has something more than the equal in another part;[1] and it is special in respect of being successive to the two sources and a system of them both.

At any rate, it is perfect in a more particular way than the other numbers to which consecutive numbers from the monad to the tetrad are found to be equal—I mean, that is, the monad, [15] triad, hexad and decad. The monad, as the basic number of this series, is equal to the monad; the triad is equal to monad and dyad; the hexad is equal to monad, dyad and triad; the decad is equal to monad, dyad, triad and tetrad. So the triad seems to have something extra in being successive to those to which it is also equal.

Moreover, they called it 'mean' and 'proportion,' not so much because it is the very first of the numbers to have a middle term, which it in particular maintains in a relation of equality to the extremes,[2] but because in the manner of equality among things of the same genus, where there is a mean between greater and less inequality of species, it too is seen as midway between more and less and has a symmetrical nature. For the number which comes before it, 2, is more than the one before *it*, and this, being double,

1. *Periisos* (more than equal) is a word made up for the similarity with *perissos* (odd); similarly for the phrase 'more than the equal'—'the equal' being the dyad, presumably. There could also be a reference to the point made in the next paragraph: the triad is 'more than just equal,' because it is also successive to the monad and the dyad.

2. I suppose this means either that 3 is 1+1+1, where the middle term is naturally equal to either of the extremes; or that in the series 1, 2, 3, the middle term is equidistant from (the arithmetic mean of) the extremes.

is the root of the basic relation of being more than; and the number
which comes after it, 4, is less than the numbers which precede *it*,
and this, being sesquialter, is the very first to have the specific
identity of the basic relation of being less than; but the triad,
between both of these, is equal to what precedes it, so it gains the
specific identity of a mean between the others.

Hence, on account of it, there are three so-called 'true' means
(arithmetic, geometric and harmonic); and three which are subcontrary to these;[3] and three terms in the case of each mean; and three
intervals (that is, in the case of each term, [16] the differences
between the small term and the mean, the mean and the large term,
and the small and the large terms); and an equal number of ratios,
according to what was said in ordering the antecedents; and
moreover three reversals appear on examination, of great to small,
great to mean, and mean to small.[4]

The monad is like a seed in containing in itself the unformed and
also unarticulated principle of every number; the dyad is a small
advance towards number, but is not number outright because it is
like a source; but the triad causes the potential of the monad to
advance into actuality and extension. 'This' belongs to the monad,
'either' to the dyad, and 'each' and 'every' to the triad. Hence we use
the triad also for the manifestation of plurality, and say 'thrice ten
thousand' when we mean 'many times many,' and 'thrice blessed.'
Hence too we traditionally invoke the dead three times. Moreover,
anything in Nature which has process has three boundaries (beginning, peak and end—that is, its limits and its middle), and two
intervals (that is, increase and decrease), with the consequence that
the nature of the dyad and 'either' manifests in the triad by means

3. The arithmetic mean between a and c is b if a-b=b-c; b is the geometric mean between a
and c if b/a=(c-b)/(b-a); b is the harmonic mean between a and c if c/a=(c-b)/(b-a). Fairly early in
the history of Greek mathematics, seven further means were distinguished. The three subcontrary means referred to are c/a=(b-a)/(c-b), which is subcontrary to the harmonic; and two which
are subcontrary to the geometric: b/a=(b-a)/(c-b) and c/b=(b-a)/(c-b).

4. A ratio is, say, 2:4, whereas the intervals mentioned just before are the differences between
any two terms in a proportion: the interval in the ratio 2:4 is 2. The 'reversals' are simply
expressing the proportions the other way round, so that, for instance, the geometric proportion
1, 2, 4 becomes 4, 2, 1, and the ratio 2:4 becomes 4:2.

of its limits.

The triad is called 'prudence' and 'wisdom'—that is, when people act correctly as regards the present, look ahead to the future, and gain experience from what has already happened in the past: so wisdom surveys the three parts of time, and consequently knowledge falls under the triad.

[17] They call the triad 'piety': hence the name 'triad' is derived from 'terror'—that is, fear and caution.[5]

From Anatolius
The triad, the first odd number, is called perfect by some, because it is the first number to signify the totality—beginning, middle and end. When people exalt extraordinary events, they derive words from the triad and talk of 'thrice blessed,' 'thrice fortunate.' Prayers and libations are performed three times. Triangles both reflect and are the first substantiation of being plane; and there are three kinds of triangle—equilateral, isosceles and scalene. Moreover, there are three rectilinear angles—acute, obtuse and right. And there are three parts of time. Among the virtues, they likened it to moderation: for it is commensurability between excess and deficiency. Moreover, the triad makes 6 by the addition of the monad, dyad and itself, and 6 is the first perfect number.

From Nicomachus' Theology
The triad is the source in actuality of number, which is by definition a system of monads. For the dyad is in a sense a monad on account of being like a source, but the triad is the first to be a system, of monad and dyad. But it is also the very first which admits of end, middle and beginning , which are the causes of all completion and perfection being attained.

The triad is the form of the completion of all things, [18] and is truly number, and gives all things equality and a certain lack of excess and deficiency, having defined and formed matter with the

5. Here *trias* (triad) is linked with *trein* (to be afraid).

potential for all qualities.[6]

At any rate, 3 is particular and special beyond all other numbers in respect of being equal to the numbers which precede it.

Those who are requesting that their prayers be answered by God pour libations three times and perform sacrifices three times; and we say 'thrice fortunate' and 'thrice happy' and 'thrice blessed' and qualify all the opposites to these as 'thrice,' in the case of those to whom each of these features is present in a perfect form, so to speak.

They say that it is called 'triad' by comparison with someone being 'unyielding'—that is, not to be worn down;[7] it gets this name because it is impossible to divide it into two equal parts.

The triad is the first plurality: for we talk of singular and dual, but then not triple, but plural, properly.[8]

The triad is pervasive in the nature of number: for there are three types of odd number—prime and incomposite, secondary and composite, and mixed, which is secondary in itself, but otherwise prime; and again, there are over-perfect, imperfect and perfect numbers; and in short, of relative quantity, some is greater, some less and some equal.

The triad is very well suited to geometry: for the basic element in plane figures is the triangle, and there are three kinds of triangle—acute-angled, obtuse-angled and scalene.

There are three configurations of the moon—waxing, full moon and waning; [19] there are three types of irregular motion of the planets—direct motion, retrogression and, between these, the stationary mode; there are three circles which define the zodiacal plane—that of summer, that of winter, and the one midway between these, which is called the ecliptic; [9] there are three kinds of living creature—land, winged and water; there are three Fates in

6. Since the triad is the first actual number, and qualities (and everything else) owe their existence to number, then the triad is the source of all qualities.

7. Here *trias* (triad) is linked with *ateires* (unyielding.)

8. Nouns and adjectives in Greek had three 'numbers': singular, dual and plural.

9. That is, the two tropics and the ecliptic: the sun's apparent path on the celestial sphere along

theology, because the whole life of both divine and mortal beings is governed by emission and receiving and thirdly requital, with the heavenly beings fertilizing in some way, the earthly beings receiving, as it were, and requitals being paid by means of those in the middle, as if they were a generation between male and female.

One could relate to all this the words of Homer, "All was divided into three,"[10] given that we also find that the virtues are means between two vicious states which are opposed both to each other and to virtue;[11] and there is no disagreement with the notion that the virtues fall under the monad and are something definite and knowable and are wisdom—for the mean is one—while the vices fall under the dyad and are indefinite, unknowable and senseless.

They call it 'friendship' and 'peace,' and further 'harmony' and 'unanimity': for these are all cohesive and unificatory of opposites and dissimilars. Hence they also call it 'marriage.' And there are also three ages in life.

the ecliptic is limited at either end by the tropics, at the points of the summer and winter solstices.

10. *Iliad* 15.189.

11. After Aristotle, the accepted analysis of the virtues (see also pp. 69, 82) was that they were each a mean between two vices at the extremes, one of which was excessive, the other defective, in relation to the mean of virtue.

On the Tetrad

[20] Everything in the universe turns out to be completed in the natural progression up to the tetrad, in general and in particular, as does everything numerical—in short, everything whatever its nature. The fact that the decad, which is gnomon and joiner,[1] is consummated by the tetrad along with the numbers which precede it,[2] is special and particularly important for the harmony which completion brings; so is the fact that it provides the limit of corporeality and three-dimensionality. For the pyramid, which is the minimal solid and the one which first appears, is obviously contained by a tetrad, either of angles or of faces, just as what is perceptible as a result of matter and form, which is a complete result in three dimensions, exists in four terms.[3]

Moreover, it is better and less liable to error to apprehend the truth in things and to gain secure, scientific knowledge by means of the quadrivium of mathematical sciences. For since all things in general are subject to quantity when they are juxtaposed and heaped together as discrete things, and are subject to size when they are combined and continuous, and since, in terms of quantity, things are conceived as either absolute or relative, and, in terms of size, as either at rest or in motion, accordingly the four mathematical systems or sciences will make their respective apprehensions in a manner appropriate to each thing: arithmetic apprehends quantity in general, but especially absolute quantity; music apprehends

---

1. Here 'gnomon' is being used primarily in its original sense as a carpenter's tool (see Glossary). As defined by Heron, however, a mathematical gnomon is that which when added to any figure or number makes the result similar to the original to which it was added; and the decad does this (see pp. 61 and 77, n. 6). The similarity between this passage and p. 109 makes me sure that a 'joiner' is also some unknown tool.

2. 1+2+3+4=10.

3. Perhaps the four Aristotelian causes, mentioned on p. 58; or perhaps the four elements (cf. Plato, *Timaeus* 32b-c, and pp. 95-6).

quantity when it is relative; and geometry apprehends size in general, but especially [21] static size; astronomy apprehends size when it is in motion and undergoing orderly change.

If number is the form of things, and the terms up to the tetrad are the roots and elements, as it were, of number, then these terms would contain the aforementioned properties and the manifestations of the four mathematical sciences—the monad of arithmetic, the dyad of music, the triad of geometry and the tetrad of astronomy, just as in the text entitled *On the Gods* Pythagoras distinguishes them as follows: "Four are the foundations of wisdom—arithmetic, music, geometry, astronomy—ordered 1, 2, 3, 4." And Cleinias of Tarentum says: "These things when at rest gave rise to arithmetic and geometry, and when moving to harmony and astronomy."

In the first place, the association of arithmetic with the monad is reasonable: for when arithmetic is abolished, so are the other sciences, and they are generated when it is generated, but not vice versa, with the result that it is more primal than them and is their mother, just as the monad evidently is as regards the numbers which follow it. But also every specific identity and property and attribute of number is found first of all in the monad, as in a seed.

The monad is in a sense quantity regarded as absolute and as the sole agent of limit and true definition; for if anything is conjoined with anything else, it cannot be alone, but must fall under the dyad, for the dyad contains the primary conception of difference. [22] And music obviously pertains to difference in some way, since it is a relation and a harmonious fitting together of things which are altogether dissimilar and involved in difference.

And geometry falls under the triad, not only because it is concerned with three-dimensionality and its parts and kinds, but also because it was characteristic of this teacher[4] always to call surfaces (which they used to term 'colors') the limiters of geometry, on the grounds that geometry concerns itself primarily with planes; but the most elementary plane is contained by a triad, either of angles or of lines; and when depth is added, from this as a base to

4. Pythagoras.

a single point, then in turn the most elementary of solids, the pyramid, is formed, which (even though in itself it is encompassed by at least four angles or surfaces) is fitted together by virtue of three equal dimensions, and these dimensions form the limits of anything subsisting in Nature as a solid.

And astronomy—the science of the heavenly spheres—falls under the tetrad, because of all solids the most perfect and the one which particularly embraces the rest by nature, and is outstanding in thousands of other respects, is the sphere, which is a body consisting of four things—center, diameter, circumference and area (i.e. surface).

Because the tetrad is like this, people used to swear by Pythagoras on account of it, obviously because they were astounded at his discovery and addressed him with devotion for it; so Empedocles says somewhere, "No, by him who handed down to our generation the tetraktys, the fount which holds the roots of ever-flowing Nature."[5] [23] For they used "ever-flowing Nature" as a metaphor for the decad, since it is, as it were, the eternal and everlasting nature of all things and kinds of thing, and in accordance with it the things of the universe are completed and have a harmonious and most beautiful limit. And its 'roots' are the numbers up to the tetrad—1, 2, 3, 4. For these are the limits and, as it were, the sources of the properties of number—the monad of sameness which is regarded as absolute, the dyad of difference and what is already relative, the triad of particularity and of actual oddness, the tetrad of actual evenness. (For the dyad is often viewed by us as being odd-like on account of being like a source, since it is not yet receptive of the pure properties of evenness and is not capable of being subdivided.)[6]

The tetrad is the first to encompass minimal and most seminal embodiment, since the most elementary body and the one with the smallest particles is fire, and this is the body whose shape as a solid

5. This couplet is generally said to be merely a traditional Pythagorean oath and is never elsewhere attributed to the authorship of Empedocles.

6. See p. 45.

is a pyramid (hence the name),[7] which alone is enclosed by four bases and four angles.

And this, we can be sure, is why there are four sources of the universe (whether, as was said before,[8] it is seen as an eternal continuum or as a created composition)—the by which, the from which, the by means of which, and the with what end (that is, God, matter, form, result).

And there are evidently also four elements (fire, air, water and earth) and their powers (heat, cold, wetness and dryness), which are disposed in things according to the nature of the tetrad.

The heavenly realm has also been arranged in the same way: for it has been assigned four centers—the one over the zenith, the one [24] at the ascendant, the one at right angles under the Earth, and the one at the descendant (which four turn out to constitute the zodiac between them); and moreover it has been assigned four limits—north, south, east and west—and, taking account of its sphericity, it has been assigned center, axis, circumference and area. Moreover, there are also this many so-called ninety-degree divisions of the zodiac, the points at which by means of the ecliptic there is contact with the four zodiacal signs in which the summer and winter solstices and the two equinoxes occur, which form a cross by being diametrically opposed. And heaven has four characteristic movements, which are interrelated and mutually dependent, and are special to it alone: forward through the mid-heaven in each latitude, <backward through the nadir>,[9] upward through something rising above the horizon, and downward through something setting.

There are four traditional seasons of the year—spring, summer, autumn and winter. And there are four measures, so to speak, of general change, of which the largest is the unbroken one called

7. *Puramis* (pyramid) is linked with *pur* (fire).

8. The current excerpt is from an unknown author, but the idea that the universe is either an eternal continuum or a created composition is superficially similar to what is said on p. 37, which is from Nicomachus.

9. There is an obvious lacuna in the text; I have filled it in with a reasonable guess. What the author seems to be referring to is nothing more than that if I stand facing east, say, then the apparent motion of any heavenly body is upward (as it rises), forward (as it passes above me), downward (as it sets) and backward (as it goes away from me under the Earth).

'eternity;' the next, 'time,' is comprehensible in itself by the mind; the next in order of subordination is 'critical time,' which is in a way accessible to apprehension by our senses; and the one which has the shortest duration and extension is 'passing time.' And from another point of view, there is year, month, night and day.

Analogously, as regards the completion of the universe, there are angels, daemons, animals and plants, which complete [25] the universe.

They even distinguish four kinds of planetary movements—progression, retrogression and two modes of being stationary, primary and secondary.[10]

There are four distinct senses in living creatures; for touch is a common background to the other four, which is why it alone does not have a location or a regular organ. There are four kinds of plants—trees, shrubs, vegetables and herbs. There are four kinds of virtues: first, wisdom in the soul and, corresponding to it, keen sensibility of the body and good fortune in external matters; second, moderation in the soul and health in the body and good repute in external matters; third, on the same arrangement, courage, strength and power; and fourth, justice, beauty and friendship.

Moreover, just as there are four seasons such as summer, so there are four seasons for man—childhood, youth, adulthood and old age.

The most elementary numerical properties are four—sameness in the monad, difference in the dyad, color in the triad[11] and solidity in the tetrad.

Man is divided into four—head, trunk, legs and arms. And there are four sources of a rational creature (as Philolaus also says in *On Nature*)—brain, heart, navel and genitals: "Head for thought, heart for soul and for feeling, navel for the embryo to take root and to grow, genitals for the emission of seed and for birth. The brain provides the source for man, the heart for [26] animals, the navel for plants, the genitals for them all: for they all both sprout and grow

10. The primary stationary mode is when a planet is changing from progresssion to retrogression, the secondary is the other way round.
11. See e.g. pp. 44 and 56 for this use of 'color.'

from seed."[12]

Even if plurality is first seen in the triad, nevertheless accretion of discrete things cannot be conceived of without the tetrad; moreover, among continuous things too, the pyramid falls under the tetrad and naturally acquires a shape which is hard to dissolve and which belongs to a body which is hard to dissolve; and accretion is in a sense the evolution of plurality, and is stronger than anything which falls under the triad.[13]

And just like Solon's apothegm about "seeing the end of a long life,"[14] it is possible to understand from Homer that those who are still alive are only thrice blessed in point of happiness, since there is still the uncertainty of change and alteration, while those who are dead have happiness securely and are out of the reach of change in a more complete manner—i.e. four-fold. For he says of someone still alive only "thrice blessed son of Atreus," but of those who have died an excellent death, "Thrice and four times blessed are the Greeks who perished then."[15]

The tetrad is the foundation of natural plurality and accretion, since the four kinds of perfection correspond and are equivalent to the four perfect numbers which subsist within the decad and are progressively equal to the numbers which run in unbroken sequence from the monad to the tetrad. For in the first place, although the monad is uncompounded, still it has a kind of perfection in [27] containing everything potentially and in lacking nothing; and besides, it gives rise to all the other numbers and gives them their specific identities regardless of what alterations differentiation has caused; and if any kind of thing is something perfect when it is equal to its parts, then even though the monad has no parts,

12. Philolaus, fragment 13 (Diels-Kranz).

13. The paragraph is a bit muddled, and perhaps the last section should follow straight on from the first. In order to understand it, it is useful to remember (see also p. 55) the distinction between things which are continuous and have size or magnitude, and those which are 'heaps' or juxtapositions of actually discrete components, and which have quantity, plurality or multitude. The things of this world are either magnitudes or multitudes, and the tetrad is being said to be responsible for both categories. Fire is the 'body which is hard to dissolve.'

14. Solon said, "Count no man happy until he is dead." See Herodotus I.30-33.

15. The first quote is perhaps from a variant of *Iliad* 3.182; the second line is *Odyssey* 5.306.

nevertheless as a whole it is equal to itself, so it would be perfect. In the second place, the triad is special in being both equal to and successive to the monad and the dyad, while it is perfect in another way and in itself, because it in particular contains beginning, middle and end. In the third place, as regards 1, 2, 3, although it is no longer successive, the hexad is equal to them and perfect in the sense that it is the first number to be equal to its own parts—a half, a third and a sixth. In the fourth place, as regards 1, 2, 3, 4, the decad, although even less successive, has acquired perfection in a different way from those other ways: for it is a measure and a complete boundary of every number, and there is no longer any natural number after it, but all subsequent numbers are produced by participation in the decad, when the cycle is started a second time, and then again and again on to infinity.[16] So here is a tetraktys[17] and this is the difference between the perfect numbers within the decad.

No doubt it is for the following reason that, while the most important and, as it were, more perfect fevers are the tertian and quartan, which are also the most easy to discern, nevertheless the quartan is the more important and the more secure, and hence harder to eliminate—because of the stability of the number 4, a stability which binds everything in a pyramidal manner [28] to secure bases.[18]

And this is why they say that Heracles, who was so steadfast, was born thanks to a tetrad.[19] Squares are, so to speak, not easy to shake from their disdain, just like Hermes, who is fashioned in this way.[20]

Since 4 is cubic and lies midway between the cubic places of the monad and the hebdomad, it is not surprising to find doctors like Hippocrates (for the hebdomad is particularly critical in illnesses)

16. See also pp. 76-7, 105, 109-10, 114.
17. The four perfect numbers, or the four types of perfection, correspond to the four levels of the tetraktys.
18. The author is bearing in mind the connection between fever and fire, and hence the pyramid (see p. 57, n. 7). On tertian and quartan fevers, see also pp. 96-9.
19. This is totally obscure. Was Heracles' birthday celebrated on the fourth of some month?
20. Square-cut statues of Hermes looked down (in disdain, our author suggests) on many road junctions.

manifestly saying that, in the real world in general, the tetrad has broad links with the hebdomad;[21] and besides, the joining of the tetrad with the hebdomad makes the decad capable of producing a fourth cubic place in the series.[22]

They used to call the tetrad 'the Nature of Aiolus,' showing the variety of what it is akin to.[23]

It is the prerequisite of the general orderliness of the universe, so they everywhere called it a 'custodian of Nature.' Poetry says that Aiolus provides the winds that give motion; and he is also called Hippotades, from the speed of the heavenly bodies which bring him to completion and because of his incessant running:[24] for Aiolus is the year, on account of the variety of things that grow year by year.

And again, they call the tetrad 'Heracles' with regard to the same notion of the year, as giving rise to duration, since eternity, time, critical time and passing time are four, as moreover are year, month, night and day, and [29] morning, midday, evening and night.

They think that the tetrad is called 'tetlad,' the enduring one,[25] by interchange of '1' with 'r,' because its square root endures the first separation from the monad;[26] and it causes all the dimensions

21. Compare Hippocrates, *Aphorisms* II.24: "In the progress of a disease, the fourth day in every seven-day period is significant."

22. This paragraph is incomprehensible without bearing in mind that here, and elsewhere in the treatise (see pp. 87, 96-9), the context is the sequences of doubles (1, 2, 4, 8, 16, 32, 64, etc.) and triples (1, 3, 9, 27, 81, 243, 729, etc.). The Pythagoreans were most impressed by the fact that in these sequences square and cube numbers occur at regular intervals—squares in the first, third, fifth, seventh, etc., places, and cubes in the first, fourth, seventh, tenth, etc., places. So "4 [sc. the fourth place] is cubic and lies mid-way between the cubic places of the monad and the hebdomad [the first and seventh places]." In each sequence, the tenth place is occupied by the fourth cube, which is a product of the cubes found in the fourth and seventh places: so "the joining of the tetrad with the hebdomad [i.e. multiplying the cubic numbers of the fourth and seventh places] makes the decad capable of producing a fourth cubic place in the series [i.e. the tenth place contains the fourth cube]."

23. Aiolus means 'the shifter.'

24. 'Hippotades' means 'son of the horseman.'

25. 'Tetlad' is a specially coined word, from *tlao* (endure).

26. See p. 42.

to subsist, or the three dimensions beyond which there are none. The Pythagoreans honored it as the begetter of the decad.

Anatolius reports that it is called 'justice,' since the square (i.e. the area) which is based on it is equal to the perimeter; for the perimeter of squares before it is greater than the area of those squares, and the perimeter of squares after it is less than the area, but in its case the perimeter is equal.[27]

The tetrad is the first to display the nature of solidity: the sequence is point, line, plane, solid (i.e. body).

Four is the first number which is even-times-even. Four is the first number which contains the sesquitertian ratio, which belongs to the primary concord, the fourth. In its case, everything is equal— area, angles, sides.[28]

There are four cardinal points; and there are four distinguishing points—ascendant, descendant, mid-heaven and nadir. The primary winds are four.

[30] Some say that all things are organized by four aspects— substance, shape, form and principle.

The tetrad comprehends the principle of soul, as well as that of corporeality; for they say that a living creature is ensouled in the same way that the whole universe is arranged, according to harmony. Perfect harmony seems to subsist in three concords: the fourth, which lies in the sesquitertian ratio; the fifth, in the sesquialter; and the octave, in double. Once there are the first four numbers—1, 2, 3, 4—then there is also the category of soul, which these numbers encompass in accordance with musical principles. For 4 is double 2 and 2 is double 1, and here is the octaval concord; 3 is one and a half times 2, a sesquialter, and here is the fifth; and 4 is sesquitertian to 3, and here is the fourth. If the universe is composed out of soul and body in the number 4, then it is also true that all concords are perfected by it.

27. See p. 44.
28. If this has any discernible sense, it is presumably that a square with area 4 has four angles and four sides, though it is difficult to see why this should be thought significant.

On the Pentad

From Anatolius

The pentad is the first number to encompass the specific identity of all number, since it encompasses 2, the first even number, and 3, the first odd number. Hence it is called 'marriage,' since it is formed of male and female. [31] It is the mid-point of the decad. When it is squared, it always encompasses itself, for 5x5=25; and when it is multiplied again, it both encompasses the square as a whole and terminates at itself, for 5x25=125.[1]

There are five solid figures with equal sides and equal angles— the tetrahedron (i.e. pyramid), octahedron, icosahedron, cube and dodecahedron. And Plato says that the first is the figure of fire, the second of air, the third of water, the fourth of earth, and the fifth of the universe.[2]

Moreover, there are five planets, not counting the sun and moon. The square on base 5 is the first to be equal to two squares—the one on base 3 and the one on base 4. A tetrachord is said to consist of the first even and the first odd number.[3] Geometric concord is thought to fall under 5.[4]

Moreover, whatever you use to add up to 10, 5, will be found to be the arithmetic mean—e.g. 9+1, 8+2, 7+3, 6+4. Each sum adds up to 10, and 5 is found to be the arithmetic mean, as the diagram

1. That is, 25 is circular, 125 is spherical.

2. See Plato, *Timaeus* 53c-56c.

3. That is, a conjunct tetrachord—a sequence of four notes made out of one set of two notes and one set of three notes, where the last of the first two and the first of the last three are the same note.

4. This is hard to understand. Is he referring to the primary geometric proportion 1, 2, 4, whose extremes add up to 5?

shows.[5]

The pentad is the first to exhibit the best and most natural mediacy, when, in conjunction with the dyad, it is taken in disjunct proportion[6] to both the limits of natural number—to the monad as source and the decad as end: [32] for as 1 is to 2, so 5 is to 10, and again as 10 is to 5, so 2 is to 1; and alternately, as 10 is to 2, 5 is to 1, and as 2 is to 10, 1 is to 5. And the product of the limits is equal to the product of the means, as is the way with geometrical proportion: for 2x5=1x10. Reciprocally, we are able to see first in the pentad, compared with the greater limit, the principle of half, just as we see this principle first in the dyad, compared with the smaller limit: for 2 is double 1, and 5 is half 10.

Hence the pentad is particularly comprehensive of the natural phenomena of the universe: it is a frequent assertion of ours that the whole universe is manifestly completed and enclosed by the decad, and seeded by the monad, and it gains movement thanks to the dyad and life thanks to the pentad, which is particularly and most appropriately and only a division of the decad, since the pentad necessarily entails equivalence, while the dyad entails ambivalence.

So there are five general elements of the universe—earth, water, air, fire and aether; and their figures are five—tetrahedron, hexahedron, octahedron, dodecahedron and icosahedron. Moreover the sum of the bases of these figures is ten times the principle of the pentad.

There are five parallel circles in the heavens: the celestial equator; the summer and winter tropics on either side of the equator, [33] which are equal to each other, but secondary in terms of size; and the circles on either side of the tropics, which define the

---

5. The diagram which would have accompanied the text is as follows:

1	4	7
2	5	8
3	6	9

6. A 'disjunct' proportion has four terms (two means), not three terms (one mean).

northern and southern elevations—the Arctic and Antarctic circles, which are smallest in size, but they too are equal to each other. And corresponding to the position of these, there are thought to be five zones on Earth too: the hot zone, corresponding to the equator; two well-blended zones, corresponding to the two tropics; and an equal number of zones which are uninhabited thanks to the cold of the poles at either end of the Earth.

There are only five planets, apart from the sun and moon. And there are this many phases of the moon, generally speaking: two when it is halved, two when it is gibbous, and one when it is full. Some people are more precise, and instead of the two halved phases put two crescent phases in the number of phases. For the moon is not really halved at the time when it is thought to be; it only appears to be halved, but it is demonstrable geometrically that it is altogether necessary for the illuminated part to be more than it appears to be and for the dark part to be less, since the sphere of the moon is smaller than that of the sun, and more than half of such a sphere is always lit up, so that the shadow cast ends up conical, and the shape which is produced in the opposite direction to the verticality of the lines of the cone is like a *calathos*; and the circular line which defines the illuminated part and the dark part circumscribes a base which is common to both shapes.[7]

There are also five contacts among the straight lines which accomplish the cosmic centers: for it is obvious that these are two diameters, which are the largest lines, intersecting each other at right angles. [34] So they touch themselves and the heavenly sphere at five points—themselves at the cosmic center, the sphere at those mentioned centers.[8]

There are this many sense-organs in more highly developed

7. A *calathos* is a basket with a narrower base than top. The diagram is as follows (see Aristarchus, *On the Sizes and Distances of the Sun and Moon*, Proposition 2):

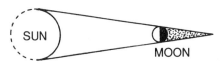

8. See p. 58 for the latter four centers.

creatures, because of kinship and similarity of arrangement and of descending order to the elements. This is why Nature separated each of the extremities of our bodily part (I mean, the extremities of our feet and hands) in a five-fold way, into fingers and toes. And there are five types of internal organ—kidneys, lung, liver, spleen and heart. And, at a general survey, there are five types of parts which are visible on the surface of the body—head, arms, trunk, genitals and legs. And there are five genera of creatures—those that live in fire, those that live in the air, those that live on earth, those that live in water and amphibious creatures.

They called the pentad 'lack of strife,' not only because aether, the fifth element, which is set apart on its own, remains unchanging, while there is strife and change among the things under it, from the moon to the Earth, but also because the primary two different and dissimilar kinds of number, even and odd, are as it were reconciled and knitted together by the pentad, which is a composite whole consisting of their conjunction, just as aether also remains reconciled to itself in shape and being and so on, and is found to provide such a property for everything else which displays all the kinds of opposition the two sources involve.

Hence Megillus too praises the pentad in his *On Numbers*, and says [35]: "The pentad is alteration, light, lack of strife: alteration because it changes three-dimensionality into the sameness of the sphere, by moving cyclically and engendering light—hence it is light too; and it is lack of strife because it combines everything which was formerly discordant, and brings together and reconciles the two types of number."[9]

The pentad is highly expressive of justice,[10] and justice comprehends all the other virtues. For justice would be what gives what is appropriate to each thing and governs equality in the soul, and

9. The pentad moves cyclically because its square, cube and so on all terminate in 5 (see Glossary under *Circular, Spherical*); this cyclical movement is above all the property of the light-bearing spheres of the heavens.

10. In earlier Pythagoreanism, the identification of the tetrad with justice (see p. 63) was standard. This is another Nicomachean excerpt.

equality is involved only in the rational part of the soul, while inequality has to do with the irrational part, unless it yields and listens to reason. But what is equal is homogeneous (for there is only one type of equality), but what is unequal is highly hetero-geneous (for there are many types of inequality) and has two primary types, greater and lesser; so also where the soul is con-cerned, there will be an equal part and an unequal part, and the equal part will be divine and rational, while the unequal part will be mortal and irrational; and the greater aspect of the unequal part is the passionate soul (for it is a boiling over and, as it were, desire to shed excess), while the lesser aspect is the appetitive soul (for it is defective because of its seeking for what is missing); but every-thing, when it is controlled by the rational part of the soul and partakes of equality on account of the rational part, gains virtue— the passionate part acquires courage, the appetitive part [36] mod-eration.[11]

So if there is any number which is equal-times-equal, then it would form and be receptive of justice. Every square number is equal-times-equal, but not every square number admits of a mean, but obviously only any one which is odd; for, as a general principle, no mean of an even number can be found.[12] And of the odd numbers the most appropriate and fitting would be the basic number of the series, since the numbers which follow it in the series admit its principles. Scientific and philosophic demonstrations always make use of the very smallest basic numbers, as both simple and trustworthy, and observe in them as paradigms the properties which they have in common with numbers of the same kind; for example, they prefer to observe in the dyad set against the monad the properties of the naturally infinite doubles, and in the triad set against the dyad the properties of sesquialters. Thus the concept and principle of justice, which is revealed in a number which is equal-times-equal (i.e. a square number), would not be correctly

11. The tripartite division of the human soul into rational, passionate and appetitive stems from Plato. A common division of soul as the life-force in general is human, animal and vegetative (see, for instance, pp. 59, 72).

12. It is assumed that a mean will play a part, since justice is a virtue and all virtues are means (see p. 53, n. 11).

revealed in an even number, since that cannot have a mean, but clearly in an odd number and, among odd numbers, in the most basic of the series—the one which is, as it were, the seed of the rest—because this is the one which is accessible to knowledge. In other words, it will be revealed first in 9; for this, being 3x3, is the basic square number of the series, since its root is the first odd number, 3 (which is the first side number with a mean), and it is the first square number to have a mean.

So we must try to adapt our account of justice to this, following [37] the Pythagorean definition of justice, which is: "The power of repayment of what is equal and appropriate, being encompassed by the mean of a square odd number."

In the first place, we must set out in a row the sequence of numbers from the monad up to it: 1, 2, 3, 4, 5, 6, 7, 8, 9. Then we must add up the amount of all of them together, and since the row contains nine terms, we must look for the ninth part of the total, to see if it is already naturally present among the numbers in the row; and we will find that the property of being the ninth belongs only to the mean itself.[13]

So, you see, the pentad is another thing which has neither excess nor defectiveness in it, and it will turn out to provide this property for the rest of the numbers, so that it is a kind of justice, on the analogy of a weighing instrument. For if we suppose that the row of numbers is some such weighing instrument, and the mean number 5 is the hole of the balance, then all the parts towards the ennead, starting with the hexad, will sink down because of their quantity, and those towards the monad, starting with the tetrad, will rise up because of their fewness, and the ones which have the advantage will altogether be triple the total of the ones over which they have the advantage, but 5 itself, as the hole in the beam, partakes of neither, but it alone has equality and sameness.

The parts adjacent to it gradually [38] decrease in advantage or disadvantage the closer they get to it, just like the parts which move away little by little from the scales on the beam towards the balance. The ennead and the monad are at the furthest distance,

13. The total is 45, and 45/9=5.

whence the ennead has the greatest advantage, the monad the greatest disadvantage, each by a full tetrad. A little further in from these are the ogdoad and dyad, whence the ogdoad has a little less excess, the dyad a little less defectiveness: in each case the excess and the defectiveness is a triad. Then, next to these, are the hebdomad and the triad, whence the triad is defective and the hebdomad excessive by the next amount—they are a dyad away from the center. Further in from these and next to the pentad, as it were to the balance, are the tetrad and the hexad, which has the least excess; for no smaller number than this can be thought of.

When the beam is suspended,[14] the parts with excess make excessive both the angle at the scales and their angle at the balance, while the parts with defectiveness make the angle defective in both cases; and the obtuse angle is the excessive one, since a right angle has the principle of maximum equality.

Since in a case of injustice those who are wronged and those who do wrong are equivalent, just as in a case of inequality the greater and the lesser parts are equivalent, but nevertheless those who do wrong are more unjust than those who suffer wrong (for the one group requires punishment, the other compensation and help), therefore the parts which are at a distance on the side of the obtuse angle, where the weighing instrument is concerned and in the terms of our mathematical illustration (i.e. the parts with advantage), are progressively [39] further away from the mean, which is justice; but the parts on the side of the acute angle will increasingly approach and come near, and as it were through continually suffering wrong in being at a disadvantage, while the others will travel downwards and into corruption and immersion in evil, they will rise up and take refuge in God through their need for retribution and compensation.

At any rate, if it is necessary, taking the beam as a whole, for

14. The type of weighing instrument Nicomachus is imagining is a hand-held one, like this:

equality to be in this mathematical illustration, then again such a
thing will be contrived thanks to the pentad's participation as it
were in a kind of justice. For one possibility is that if all the parts
which are arranged at a fifth remove from the excessive parts are
subtracted from them and added to the disadvantaged parts, then
what is being sought will be the result.[15]

Alternatively, thanks to the pentad's being a point of distinction
and reciprocal separation, if the disadvantaged one which is closest
to the balance on that side is subtracted from the one which is
furthest from the balance on the excessive side and added to the one
which is furthest from the balance on the other side (i.e. 1)—if, to
effect equalization, 4 is subtracted from 9 and added to 1; and from
8, 3 is subtracted, which will be the addition to 2; and from 7, 2 is
subtracted, which is added to 3; and from 6, 1 is subtracted, which
is the addition to 4 to effect equalization; then all of them equally,
both the ones which have been punished, as excessive, and the ones
which have been set right, as wronged, will be assimilated to the
mean of justice. For all of them will be 5 each; and 5 alone remains
unsubtracted and unadded, so that it is neither more nor less, but
it alone encompasses by nature what is fitting and appropriate.

Those who first formed the characters of the letters [40] in terms
of shape—since θ signifies nine, and the mean of it as a square is ε,
and the mean in nearly very case is seen as half—considered that ε
formed half of the letter θ, as if it were cut into two.[16]

Because in this way justice is most justly seen in the number 5,
and the arithmetical image of a 'row' is not implausibly likened to
a beam, Pythagoras produced in the form of a maxim for those who
know the instruction "Do not overstep a beam," i.e. justice. [17]

Since in the realm of embodiment there are, according to natural
scientists, three life-engendering things—vegetative, animal and
rational—and since the rational is subsumed under the hebdomad

15. Equality is "what is being sought": "all the parts which are at a fifth remove from the
excessive parts" are 1, 2, 3, 4—respectively at a fifth remove from 6, 7, 8, 9. So if the sum of 1,
2, 3, 4,—i.e. 10—is subtracted from the sum of 6, 7, 8, 9, and added to the sum of 1, 2, 3, 4, the
result is equality: 20=20.
16. See p. 39, n. 15. The letter θ (theta) was the symbol for 9, ε (epsilon) for 5. Nicomachus
is here imagining θ cut in half down the vertical axis.
17. There are many extant Pythagorean maxims, some of which are equally banal, at first sight
(e.g. "Put your right shoe on first," "Don't stir fire with a knife"), and were therefore open to

and the animal under the hexad, then the vegetative necessarily falls under the pentad, with the result that the pentad is the minimal extreme of life. For the monad is the root of all generations, and the dyad is change in respect of a single dimension, the triad in respect of a second dimension, the tetrad in respect of a third and more complete dimension; and the pentad is change in respect of all addition and increase, which falls under the vegetative aspect of the soul, in which (it goes without saying) perception in general is also interspersed.[18]

They call the pentad 'Nemesis.' At any rate, it distributes[19] the heavenly and divine and physical elements by means of five;[20] it distributes the five forms to the cyclical movements both of the moon and of the rest of the heavenly bodies—the movements being evening setting, evening [41] rising, dawn setting, dawn rising, and simple revolution which involves no setting or rising; moreover it distributes those heavenly bodies which are on epicycles to two stationary modes, or to progression, or to retrogression, and those which are not to one natural regularity.[21]

The general structure of plants is five-fold—root, stem, bark, leaf and fruit. And there are five precipitations—of rain, snow, dew, hail and frost—and five exhalations—steam, smoke, fog, mist and the so-called whirlwind, which some call 'cyclone.' This is why another word for pentad is 'pempad,' because these movements are sent upwards[22] and are subsumed under the pentad.

Because it levels out inequality, they call it 'Providence' and 'justice' (division, as it were),[23] and 'Bubastian' because of being honored at Bubastos in Egypt,[24] and 'Aphrodite' because it binds to

allegorical interpretation.

18. The schema is possibly derived from Philolaus (see further pp. 66, 93, 103): (1) point, (2) line, (3) plane, (4) solid, (5) vegetative increase of solid bodies, (6) animal soul and its faculties, (7) rational soul and its faculties, (8) suprarational faculties. What were 9 and 10?

19. *Nemein* (distribute) is the root of 'Nemesis.'

20. Earth, water, air, fire, aether.

21. The theory of epicycles was a way of explaining the four apparently irregular motions of the planets; the sun and moon, however, have regular motion.

22. The root of the word translated 'sent' is -*pemp*-.

23. The word for 'division' (*dichesis*) is similar to that for 'justice' (*dike*); see also p. 46, n. 12.

24. Bubastis was an Egyptian deity, identified with Isis or, in the Roman system, Diana; the place here called 'Bubastos' was the town around her temple.

each other a male and female number.[25] Likewise, it is called 'nuptial' and 'androgyny' and 'demigod'—the latter not only because it is half of ten, which is divine, but also because in its special diagram it is assigned the central place.[26] And it is called 'twin' because it divides in two the decad, which is otherwise indivisible; and 'immortal' and 'Pallas,' because it reveals the fifth essence;[27] and 'heart-like' because of the analogy of the heart being assigned the center in living creatures.

From the Second Discourse, on the Pentad, of the Arithmetic *of Nicomachus of Gerasa*[28]

[42] When men are wronged, they want the gods to exist, but when they commit wrong, they do not want the gods to exist; hence they are wronged so that they may want the gods to exist. For if they do not want the gods to exist, they do not persevere. Therefore, if the cause of men's perseverance is their wanting the gods to exist, and if they want gods to exist when they are wronged, and if wrong, though an evil, still looks to Nature's advantage, and whatever looks to Nature's advantage is good, and Nature is good, and Providence is the same, then evil happens to men by Providence. It is likely that the origins of this too were given by Homer, when he says:[29]

> And then the father stretched out golden scales
> And put in two portions of death which causes long grief,
> One for the horse-taming Trojans, one for the bronze-armoured
>   Greeks;
> And he pulled the scales up by the middle, and the death-day of the
>   Greeks was heavier.
> The portions of the Greeks settled on to the fertile earth,
> While those of the Trojans rose up towards the broad sky.

---

25. See p. 65.

26. See p. 66, n. 5.

27. Pallas is Athena; fifth essence, or quintessence, is æther.

28. That is, from Nicomachus' *Theology of Arithmetic*; this extraordinary appendix is prompted by the image of justice and the scales of pp. 68-72.

29. *Iliad* 8.69-74.

On the Hexad

From Anatolius

The hexad is the first perfect number; for it is counted by its own parts, as containing a sixth, a third and a half. When squared, it includes [43] itself, for 6x6=36; when cubed, it no longer maintains itself as a square, for 6x36=216, which includes 6, but not 36.[1]

It arises out of the first even and first odd numbers, male and female, as a product and by multiplication; hence it is called 'androgynous.' It is also called 'marriage,' in the strict sense that it arises not by addition, as the pentad does, but by multiplication. Moreover, it is called 'marriage' because it is equal to its own parts, and it is the function of marriage to make offspring similar to parents.

The harmonic mean is first formed by the hexad, since the sesquitertian ratio of 8 set against 6, and the double ratio of 12 set against 6, are both gained.[2] For by the same fraction, namely a third, 8 both exceeds and is exceeded by the extremes. The arithmetic mean also falls under 6, since the sesquialter ratio of 9 set against it, and the double ratio of 12 set against it, are both gained. For by the same number, 3, 9 both exceeds one extreme and is exceeded by the other. Moreover, its parts (namely, 1, 2, 3) have a certain arithmetical proportion. Moreover, 6 forms a geometric mean—3, 6, 12.

Moreover, there are six [44] extensions of solid bodies.[3]

After the pentad, they used naturally to praise the number 6 in very vivid eulogies, concluding from unequivocal evidence that the

---

1. That is, 36 is circular, 216 is spherical.

2. As a matter of fact, however, the primary harmonic proportion was usually regarded as 3, 4, 6, not 6, 8, 12.

3. That is, the six directions: forward, backward, up, down, left, right.

universe is ensouled and harmonized by it and, thanks to it, comes
by both wholeness and permanence, and perfect health, as regards
both living creatures and plants in their intercourse and increase,
and beauty and excellence, and so on and so forth. They undertook
to prove this by adducing the following as evidence: the disorder
and (in so far as it itself is concerned) formlessness of the eternal
prime matter, and lack of absolutely everything which makes for
distinctness (in respect of quality and quantity and all the other
categories),[4] was separated out and made orderly by number, since
number is the most authoritative and creative kind of thing, and
matter in fact partakes of distinctness and regulated alteration and
pure coherence thanks to its desire for and imitation of the properties of number.

But number itself is found to have formed its progression to
infinity by means of the hexad, in perfect additions.[5] For primary
perfection is having beginning, middle and end, and secondary
perfection is being equal to one's own parts, without excess or
deficiency in being related to them; and the primary type is found
in the triad, as in a root, and the secondary type is found in the
hexad, as the basic number of the series of numbers which have this
type of perfection; but the triad's perfection is also found contin-
gently in the hexad (for 2+2+2 is again beginning, middle and end),
but the hexad's perfection is not to be found in the triad (for its parts
are defective in relation to the whole); and we find that, by nature
and not by our own hypotheses, quantities occur in triads and that
in the adding of numbers these quantities give the total aggregate,
right up to infinity, a hexadic identity. For the first triad of
quantities, 1, 2, 3, is given its identity by the hexad itself; and the
second quantities, 4, 5, 6, are again given their identity by a hexad,
when [45] a single monad recurs by starting the cycle again at the
next stage; and the subsequent quantities, 7, 8, 9, are again given
their identity by a hexad, when *two* monads are reproduced; and the
same goes when three and four and subsequent triads—10, 11, 12

4. The ten Aristotelian categories are substance (or being), quantity, quality, relation, place,
time, situation, having, doing, and being done to.

5. That is, as emerges from what follows, additions which involve triads and hexads, which
have the two primary types of perfection.

and so on, as far as you like—are added up, with the result that it turns out that all number is formed by the dependence of triad on hexad; and since number is formative of the formlessness in matter, we would not be wrong in considering the hexad to be the form of forms.[6]

From another point of view, if the soul gives articulation and composition to the body, just as soul at large does to formless matter, and if no number whatsoever can be more suited to the soul than the hexad, then no other number could be said to be the articulation of the universe, since the hexad is found stably to be maker of soul and causer of the condition of life (hence the word 'hexad').[7]

That all soul is harmonic and that the most elementary concordant intervals are the sesquitertian and sesquialter, by the combination of which all the other intervals are filled, is clear. For when soul is present, the opposites which have been admitted by the living creature are reconciled and ordered and tuned as well as possible, as they yield and correspond to each other and hence cause health in the compound—the opposites being hot and cold, wet and dry, heavy and light, compact and loose, and so on, [46] which would not exist together without some harmony; assuredly, in so far as soul is present, they can congregate, but when soul departs, then dissolution and desertion of all the components of the creature occur. Moreover, the mentioned elementary sources of harmony— the sesquialter and the sesquitertian—need a half (for the sesquialter cannot exist without this, nor indeed can the musical fifth, which the sesquialter forms) and a third (for the sesquitertian is altogether bound up with this, and the musical fourth is naturally bound up with the sesquitertian); and 6 is the first number to subsume both a half and a third at once, since it is made up of different and contrary factors—the root of things which are divis-

6. This paragraph takes for granted what is more clearly stated by Iamblichus, *On Nicomachus' Introduction to Arithmetic* 103.10-104.13 (readily accessible in Thomas, pp. 106-9). The "next stage" is to treat 10 as 1, since it starts the next cycle of ten numbers: this is what is here called "the single monad recurring." Thus the sum of 4, 5 and 6, which is 15, may be treated as the sum of 1 and 5, which is 6; the sum of 7, 8 and 9 is 24, which may be regarded as 2+4; and so on. See also pp. 61, 105, 109-10, 114.

7. The word 'hexad' is here derived from *hexis* (condition).

ible by two, and the root of things which are divisible by three, the dyad and the triad—so that, just as there occurs in it the association of things which are altogether at variance, so the hexad is constituted to bring together and into unison things which are altogether different.

And since, as we said earlier,[8] it is also necessary for the largest class of soul to be a solid number—spherical, in fact, and not solid only in a male or only in a female way, but in both ways (for vitality is common equally to both species)—and since, in this context, 6 is the first to contain the principle of even-odd nature,[9] then what is spherical in accordance with it, and not with the pentad, is considered to be more suited to the soul, inasmuch as it is androgynous, while 5 has only one or the other identity.[10]

Again, solidity turns out to fall under six and to be not single, but triple: for the square based on a six-foot side is the summation of the cube of odd and even in potential, and at the same time of the cube of each in actuality—$1+8+27=36$.[11]

Apart from this sum, 36 encompasses harmony as well: [47] for it is also the sumation of 6, 8, 9 and 12 (and their common source, which is the monad), and these are the numbers in which the musical intervals which most properly constitute harmony in general are said by musicians to reside: the double of the octave lies in the extremes; the sesquialter of the fifth lies in each mean being related in turn to the extremes, a different one in each case—12 to the one which is not next to it in the series, i.e. to 8, and 9 not to 8, but to 6; and the sesquitertian of the fourth lies likewise in the means being taken in relation to the extremes, but this time to the ones which are adjacent in the series, not to the ones which are discontinuous—i.e. 8 to 6 and 9 to 12.

That the hexad is particularly responsible for this is clear: for it

8. Where? This appears to be a careless take-over by the compiler of our treatise from his source, who from the break in the text on p. 75 has probably been Nicomachus.

9. Because it is made up of the first male and first female numbers, 3 and 2.

10. The spherical number based on 6 is 216: the relation of this to soul or life is explained on pp. 83-4, 93-4.

11. Remember that 1 is 'odd and even in potential.' Six informs *solidity* because its square is the sum of these basic *cubes.*

subsists as the basis of all the concords, since it occupies the place of the lowest string of the tetrachord, and from it as base all the intervals are mapped out.[12]

If we employ a more scientific approach in arranging the embodiment of the soul, and not only regard it as something three-dimensional, but also consider that it is necessary for each dimension to be bounded on both sides, we will conceive of two boundaries for each, and since there are three dimensions, the result will be six boundaries, which is why the so-called bodily directions[13] are also this many, seen as two for each dimension, with the result that this solid embodiment of the soul also falls under the hexad.

Moreover, this is also why there are six so-called true means (which some call proportions), and this many simple ways of being unequal,[14] to which are assigned all the irrational parts, both of all other things and of the soul itself, which admit commensuration and equalization. For the hexad is the first and most basic number to encompass [48] an arithmetic mean; for since the arithmetic mean is obviously contained primarily in 1, 2, 3, and the combination of these is the hexad, then the hexad admits the primary expression of proportionality and forms number itself, since the characteristic property of being a numerical mean is found essentially in it;[15] and also the primary embodiment of scalene number is solidified in the sequence up to it—1, 2, 3.

The Pythagoreans, following Orpheus, called the hexad 'wholeness of limbs,' either because it alone of the numbers within the decad is a whole equal to its parts or limbs,[16] or because the whole—

12. Imagine numbering the strings on a four-stringed instrument 6, 8, 9, 12.

13. See pp. 75, n. 3, and 81, n. 27.

14. On the three true means and their three subcontraries, see p. 50, n. 3. Greek mathematicians distinguished ten forms of inequality. The six 'simple' ones are presumably being multiples and submultiples, superparticulars and subsuperparticulars, superpartients and subsuperpartients. For multiples and submultiples, see the Glossary. Superparticular numbers are of the form $1+1/n$ (so both sesquialters and sesquitertians are superparticulars); subsuperparticulars have the form of $n/(n+1)$. Superpartients have the form $1+m/(m+n)$; subsuperpartients have the form $(m+n)/(2m+n)$.

15. The arithmetic mean is characteristic of number because any number can be defined as half the sum of the two on either side of it (and of the next two, etc.).

16. The Greek for 'part' is *meros*, for 'limb' *melos*.

that is, the universe—has been divided into parts and is harmonious thanks to it:[17] for since there are seven celestial movements
(apart from the movement of the fixed stars, which is eighth, but
complex), and since by their hurtling they produce the same
number of notes, then their intervals and, as it were, means are
necessarily six.[18]

They rightly call it 'reconciliation': for it weaves together male
and female by blending, and not by juxtaposition as the pentad
does.[19] And it is plausibly called 'peace,' and a much earlier name
for it, based on the fact that it organizes things, was 'universe':[20] for
the universe, like 6, is often seen as composed of opposites in
harmony, and the summation of the word 'universe' is 600.[21]

They also called it 'health' and 'anvil' (as it were, the unwearying
one),[22] because it is reasonable to think that the most fundamental
triangles of the elements of the universe partake in it, since each
triangle is six, if it is divided by three perpendiculars: for it would
be divided altogether into six parts.[23] That is why there are [49] as
many edges to a pyramid as there are, and as many faces of a cube,
and as many angles in an octahedron and bases of a dodecahedron
and edges to a cube and an octahedron and an icosahedron, and
nothing pertaining to their faces or angles or edges is altogether free
from the hexad.[24]

There are also six signs of the zodiac over the Earth and six under
the Earth.

Progression from the monad to the pentad is straightforward, but
from the hexad the progression finds another starting-point and is

17. 'Harmonious' translates *emmeles*, while the Greek for limb is *melos*.

18. This is the famous theory of the 'harmony of the spheres'—that as the seven planets move
around the Earth, the notes they each emit make up a cosmic harmony. See also pp. 99, 104.

19. See pp. 75, 78.

20. *Kosmos* (universe) literally means 'order.'

21. See p. 39, n. 15: *kosmos* adds up to 600.

22. The Greek words for 'anvil' and 'unwearying' are superficially similar.

23. On these triangles, their relation to the elements, and the elements' relation to the regular
solids, see Plato, *Timaeus* 53c-57d, and p. 115.

24. All the things mentioned are either six or multiples of six: a pyramid has six edges; a cube
has six faces and twelve edges; an octahedron has twelve edges and twenty-four angles; and so
on.

repetitive: for one and five make the next number in the sequence, 6, and two and five make the one after that, then three and five next, then four and five, then finally five take twice, by means of five having the same relationship to itself.

They also called it 'hurler of missiles,' 'presider over crossroads' and 'measurer of time in twos'—'hurler of missiles' from it being generated by the triad, which tradition tells us is Hecate, when the triad is hurled (and, as it were, added) on to itself;[25] 'presider over crossroads' perhaps from the nature of the goddess,[26] but probably because the hexad is the first to acquire the three movements of the dimensions, and each movement is two-fold, being bounded on both sides by boundaries;[27] 'measurer of time in twos' because of the distribution of all time, which is accomplished by a hexad of zodiacal signs over the Earth and another under the Earth, or because time, since it has three parts,[28] is assimilated to the triad, and the hexad arises from two threes.

This latter reason is also why they called it 'Amphitrite,' because it yields from itself two separate triads: for 'separate' is 'apart,' through being divided into two.[29]

The simple idea that the hexad [50] is a very close neighbor of the pentad led to them attributing to it the title 'dweller by justice.'[30]

It is also called 'Thaleia' because of its harmonizing different things,[31] and 'panacea,' either because of its connection with health, which we mentioned earlier,[32] or as it were self-sufficiency, because it has been furnished with parts sufficient for wholeness.[33]

25. 'Hurler of missiles,' a Homeric epithet of Apollo, is in Greek *hekatebeletis*, so it is here derived from 'Hecate' and the root *-bal-*, meaning 'hurl.'

26. 'Presider over crossroads' was a title of Hecate.

27. 'Crossroads' in Greek is literally 'the meeting of *three* ways.' The relation of the six movements to the three dimensions is as follows: forward and backward are in the dimension of length; up and down are in the dimension of depth; right and left are in the dimension of breadth.

28. Past, present and future.

29. Amphitrite was Poseidon's wife; her name is here derived from *amphis* (separate) and 'triad.'

30. See pp. 68-72 for the relation between the pentad and justice.

31. Thaleia (the plentiful one) was the name both of one of the Muses and of one of the Graces.

32. In our treatise, however, only the mere fact that it is called 'health' is mentioned (p. 80).

33. That is, it is a perfect number; *panarkeia*, a made-up word for 'self-sufficiency,' is similar to 'panacea.'

*

Since there are seven celestial spheres, the intervals fall under the hexad: for they are always less by a monad. And there are six bases which are the boundaries of the three dimensions of a cube— i.e. of corporeality.

Because the perfection of the universe falls under the hexad, the virtue of the Creator God is rightly thought to be hexadic. For alone among all the virtues, wisdom is a divine and perfect true extreme—that is, it is not a mean, but has just one thing simply opposed to it (its lack, ignorance) which is not opposed by excess or deficiency.[34] Nor is wisdom absent from any other virtue, but it accompanies all of them, since they are mortal;[35] and it is thanks to this virtue alone, which because of its participation in the hexad has neither excess nor deficiency in relation to its parts, but altogether has equality and consequent perfection and wholeness, that the universe is not excessive, in so far as it was fashioned by the wisdom and providence of God and has been occupied by this virtue, both it and, as regards its parts, plants and animals, as will also appear in our discussion of the hebdomad.[36]

Now, inasmuch as it is relevant to the hexad, we must briefly see what is the result of forming the sequence which starts with the monad in the Pythagorean right-angled triangle: first, there is the one actual right angle in it, while there are two angles which are unequal to each other, but both together are equal to the previously mentioned angle, just as both the squares formed on each of the sides which subtend these two angles are equal to the square based on the line which subtends the right angle; three is the quantity [51] of the smaller of the two sides which contain the right angle, four the quantity of the larger one, five the quantity of the hypotenuse, and six the quantity of the area, i.e. of half of the parallelogram, which half is defined by the diagonal of the parallelogram.[37]

The sequence from the monad to the hexad is continuous; music

34. See p. 53, n. 11.

35. They are virtues of mortal parts of the soul (see pp. 68-9).

36. It is difficult to find this in the section on the hebdomad: the compiler has slipped up again.

37. Since this paragraph leads straight into the psychogony of the next, it is relevant to refer to Adam for the relation of the Pythagorean triangle to psychogony and the viability of embryos.

starts with the hexad and proceeds by doubles and triples; and the harmonious adaptation which it crucial for all things, and pertains to the viability of seven-month and especially nine-month children, starts with these musical sequences. For whether (in accordance with the two vital tributaries, double and triple) the sequence based on the hexad were to proceed doubly by means of twelve, or triply by means of eighteen, each interval would be filled in such a way that the sequence would contain two means, the first exceeding one extreme in the same proportion as it is exceeded by the other, the second exceeding one extreme by the same number as it is exceeded by the other,[38] with the result that the sequence would admit the ratios both of sesquialter and sesquitertian intervals, and in either case the engendering of living creatures, which is what we are trying to explain, will completely occur. For in the double sequence of 6 and 12, where 8 and 9 occupy the means (and patently accomplish what has been said),[39] 35, the addition of all the numbers together, when multiplied by the hexad, results in the seven-month period of 210 days; and in the triple sequence of 6 and 18, where 9 and 12 are intercalated and yield in their turn the same harmonic relation, the addition of these numbers makes 45, which multiplied again by the hexad yields the number of 9 months, i.e. 270 days; the result is that both these periods which engender living creatures depend on the hexad, which is then soul-like.[40]

At any rate, in Plato the first portion in the generation of soul [52] is very reasonably held to be the hexad, and then there is its double, 12, and its triple, 18, and so on up to 162, 27 times the first.[41] For these are the first and least quantities in which is seen the nature of the two means and that of the sesquioctaval interval in between both.[42]

Since the cube of 6 is 216, the period pertaining to seven-month offspring, when to the seven months are added the six days in which

38. See Plato, *Timaeus* 36a, which is partially quoted here; the first mean is harmonic, the second arithmetic.

39. See p. 78.

40. On seven-month and nine-month gestation, see also pp. 93-4; it is a recurring theme in ancient arithmology.

41. Compare Plato, *Timaeus* 35b-c; and pp. 84-5.

42. 4/3 : 3/2 = 9/8.

the seed froths up and germinates,[43] then Androcydes the Pythagorean, who wrote *On the Maxims*, and Eubulides the Pythagorean, Aristoxenus, Hippobotus and Neanthes, who all recorded Pythagoras' deeds, said that the transmigrations of soul which he underwent occurred at 216-year intervals; that after this many years, at all events, he came to reincarnation and rebirth as Pythagoras, as it were after the first cycle and return of the soul-generating cube of six (and this number is in fact recurrent because of being spherical), and that he was born at other times after these intervals. This is consistent with him having had the soul of Euphorbus during that period:[44] for there are about 514 years of history from the Trojan War until the time of Xenophanes the natural scientist and Anacreon and Polycrates and the siege and dislocation of the Ionians by Harpagus the Mede, which the Phocians fled and then founded Massilia; and Pythagoras [53] was contemporary with all of this. At any rate, it is recorded that, when Cambyses took Egypt, Pythagoras was taken prisoner by him (for he was living with the priests), and went to Babylon and was initiated into the non-Greek mysteries; and Cambyses was exactly contemporary with Polycrates' tyranny, which Pythagoras was fleeing from when he went to Egypt. So when twice the period has been subtracted (i.e. twice 216 years), 82 years are left for his life.

Since the nature of the number 6 is in a sense crucial for the generation and formation of soul, then what Plato says will be found helpful, as follows: the compound structure, from which is dispensed the generation of soul and from which are separated the portions up to 27 times the first, is hexadic according to Plato too, since he focuses on precisely the property we have attributed to the hexad.[45] For since the hexad is not only a clear likeness, more than

43. Greek months consisted of thirty days. The first six days of pregnancy were commonly held to be different from the rest, a preliminary period leading to pregnancy proper (see also pp. 93-4). Interestingly, in modern embryology, the fertilized egg is reckoned to be implanted in the uterus on or about the sixth day.

44. Pythagoras claimed to be a reincarnation of Euphorbus, a Trojan at the time of the Trojan War.

45. As a matter of fact, in *Timaeus* 35b-c Plato says nothing about the hexad: here our unknown source is justifying interpreting Plato as talking covertly about the hexad (this interpretation, it should be said, is not entirely implausible).

any other number, of the even-odd monad, because it is the very
first to contain parts with opposite names and opposite denomina-
tions (for its third is 2, its half 3, its sixth 1, and the whole is 6), but
also because it is a compound of the first actual odd number and the
first actual even number at once, and for this reason it alone of all
numbers within the decad is half even, half odd, and is therefore
patently a mixture of indivisible being and divisible being; and
since it is more directly oblong than any number (for it is unreason-
able to consider the dyad as oblong);[46] and since in addition it has
been discovered to be the first solid number (even if scalene,
nevertheless it is three-dimensional because of its means);[47] and
since it is the smallest of all the numbers which fall under it [54] and
are completely counted by their own parts[48] —for all these reasons,
Plato blended the mixture in a reasonable way (the first ingredient
being indivisible being, the second divisible being, and the third the
being which consists of both together, so that two things may each
be three-fold, or, conversely, three things two-fold), as being equal
to 2x3 or 3x2, odd and even and even-odd.

That it is impossible to find within the hexad another number
which admits all the ratios of the harmony of the soul, is also shown
by Aristaeus the Pythagorean.

46. The dyad could be seen as oblong if, as it were, a linear array of dots were seen not only
to have length, but also breadth: in this way a linear array of n dots would form an oblong of sides
n and one. This was, in fact, an alternative way of viewing numbers in Greek times (hence the
contentious tone of the parenthesis). Our author does not want to regard the dyad as oblong, but
in that case it should be prime; yet throughout our treatise the threefold classification of odd
numbers is adopted which excludes 2 from being prime (see Glossary under *Linear, Prime*). The
solution to this tension is simply to regard 2 not as an actual number, but as a source of number
(see the section on the dyad, *passim*), in which case it is not actually oblong, or actually prime,
or actually anything.

47. See p. 79 and Glossary under *Scalene*. There are two means to any solid number (see Plato,
Timaeus 32a-b).

48. i.e. perfect numbers.

On the Heptad

From Anatolius

Seven is not born of any mother and is a virgin.[1] The sequence from the monad to it added together totals 28; the 28 days of the moon are fulfilled hebdomad by hebdomad.

Starting with the monad and making a sequence by doubling, seven numbers yield 64, the first square which is also a cube: 1, 2, 4, 8, 16, 32, 64. Doing the same, but trebling, seven numbers yield 729, [55] the second square-and-cube: 1, 3, 9, 27, 81, 243, 729.

Moreover, the hebdomad consisting of the three dimensions (length, breadth and depth) and the four limits (point, line, surface and solid) reveals corporeality.

Seven is said to be the number of the primary concord, the fourth (4:3), and of geometric proportion (1, 2, 4). It is also called 'that which brings completion;'[2] for seven-month children are viable. The hebdomad is critical in illnesses. Seven encompasses the sides around the right angle of the archetypal right-angled triangle: the length of one is 4, of the other 3. There are seven planets.

We see seven things—body, distance, shape, size, color, movement and rest. There are seven movements—up, down, forward, backward, right, left and circular. Plato composed the soul out of seven numbers.[3] Everything is fond of sevens. There are seven vowels and seven alterations of voice.[4] There are 7 ages, as Hippocrates says:[5]

Seven are the seasons, which we call ages—child, boy, adolescent,

1. See pp. 90, 99.

2. This is also a priest's title, meaning 'initiator.'

3. See *Timaeus* 35d.

4. That is, seven ways in which any of the vowels can be sounded: with an acute, grave or circumflex accent; aspirated or unaspirated; long or short.

5. *On Hebdomads* 5.

youth, man, elder, old man.[56] One is a child up to the shedding
of teeth, until seven years; a boy up to puberty, until twice 7; an
adolescent up to the growth of the beard, until three times 7; a
youth during the general growth of the body, until four times 7;
a man up to one short of fifty years, until seven times 7; an
elder up to 56 years, until seven times 8; from then on one is an
old man.

From the Second Book of the Arithmetic *of Nicomachus of Gerasa*[6]
It is called 'forager,'[7] because its structure has been collected and
gathered together in a manner resembling unity, since it is altogether indissoluble, except into something which has the same
denominator as itself;[8] or because all things have brought their
natural results to completion by its agency; or rather (what is more
Pythagorean) because the most eminent Babylonians, and Hostanes and Zoroaster, authoritatively call the heavenly [57] spheres
'flocks,'[9] either in so far as, alone among corporeal magnitudes,
they are completely drawn around a single center, or because their
connections are decreed even by scientific savants to also in a sense
be called 'clusters;' and they for the same reason call these clusters
'flocks' in their holy writings, and also 'angels' by insertion of the
lost 'g;'[10] hence the heavenly bodies and spirits which are outstanding in each of these flocks are likewise called angels and archangels,
and they are seven in number, with the consequence that the
hebdomad is in this respect most truly a message.[11]

Moreover, it is called 'guardian' for the same reason: for not only
will there be seven leaders in addition to the number of the guards,[12]
but also those which guard the universe and keep it in continuous
and eternal stability are this many heavenly bodies.

*

6. Nicomachus' lost *Theology of Arithmetic*, as usual.
7. An epithet of Athena, with whom the hebdomad is commonly identified.
8. That is, 1/7.
9. The Greek for 'forager' is *agelaia*, for 'flock' *agele*.
10. The Greek for 'flock' may also be *agelos*; the Greek for 'angel' is *aggelos*.
11. The Greek for 'message' is *aggelia*, what angels bring; Nicomachus means us to remember *agelaia* (forager).
12. A reference to Homer, *Iliad* 9.85, or to some allegorical interpretation of it.

The Pythagoreans say that the heptad is not similar to the other numbers, and they say that it deserves reverence; and indeed they call it 'septad,'[13] as Prorus the Pythagorean also records in his *On the Hebdomad*. Hence too when they say 'six,' they stress the pronunciation of the 'k' and the 's' (for these are heard together in the 'x'), so that when they go through the successive numbers step by step, the 's' joins on to the 'seven.' So it was imperceptibly pronounced 'septa.'[14]

The reason for the seventh number being an object of reverence is as follows: the providence of the Creator God [58] wrought all things by basing on the first-born One the source and root of the creation of the universe, which comes to be an impression and representation of the highest good, and he located the perfection and fulfillment of completion in the decad itself, and the Creator God necessarily considered that the hebdomad was an instrument and his most authoritative limb and has gained the power of creativity. For by nature, and not by our own devices, the hebdomad is a mean between the monad and the decad,[15] and the means between extremes are in a sense more authoritative than the extremes themselves, because the terms on either side incline towards the means. Not only do 4 and 7 mediate between the monad and the decad by an arithmetically equal relationship, and when added together their sum is equal to the sum of the extremes, and 4 exceeds one by the same amount that 7 is less than ten, and conversely 4 is less than 10 by the same amount that 7 exceeds 1— not only this, but also the numbers from the monad to the tetrad are potentially ten, while the decad is this very thing in actuality, and 7 is the arithmetic mean between the tetrad and the decad (i.e. in a sense between two decads, one potential, the other actual), since it is half of the sum of both.[16]

Moreover, the hebdomad seems to be an acropolis, as it were, and

---

13. A word coined for its similarity with the Greek for 'reverence.'

14. The Greek for 'six' is *hex*, for 'seven' *hepta*. So they ran the s-sound at the end of *hex* on to the beginning of *hepta*.

15. That is, as what follows shows, a mean in the disjunct proportionate series 1, 4, 7, 10.

16. Note also that 28 is the seventh triangular number, 55 is the tenth triangular number, and 28 is the arithmetic mean between 1 and 55.

a 'strong fortification' within the decad, just like an indivisible monad. For it alone admits no breadth, since it is a rectilinear number and admits only a fractional part with the same denominator as itself; and, by mingling with any of the numbers within the decad, it does not produce any of the numbers within the decad, nor is it produced by the intercourse of any of the numbers within the decad, but, with a principle which is all its own and [59] is not shared, it has been assigned the most critical place.

Hence many things, both in the heavens of the universe and on the Earth—celestial bodies and creatures and plants—are in fact brought to completion by it. And that is why it is called 'Chance,' because it accompanies everything which happens, and 'critical time,' because it has gained the most critical position and nature.

The facts of the heavenly spheres provide important proof of this thesis, in that the sphere of the moon, which is the eighth from the top and the third from the bottom, carries the influence and power of the influences which revolve around the Earth, since it is considered to be the mediator between those above and those below.[17] And it turns out to employ a hebdomad for this, with a tetrad assisting as shield-bearer—for the tetrad, along with the hebdomad itself, is evidently a mean in the decad, with the result that necessarily completion and fulfillment are achieved for things by means of both numbers, especially given that 28, which is perfect in relation to its parts, is the product of the multiplication of them both (for it is four times seven)—but the hebdomad's assistance is far greater: for the addition of the numbers from the monad to the hebdomad yields 28. So the four phases of the moon each last for a seven-fold season [60] and reasonably complete the month of this heavenly body, which consists of just about 28 days.

It is also necessary to calculate the seven configurations of the moon which pertain to its phases by means of a tetrad: sickle, halved, gibbous, full—and again gibbous (when it is illuminated on the other side), and again halved (for the same reason) and again

17. The ten heavenly spheres in the Pythagorean system are: the fixed stars, Saturn, Jupiter, Mars, Sun, Venus, Mercury, Moon, Earth and Counter-Earth. (The Counter-Earth is an invisible counterpart to the Earth. It is the body closest to the central fire or hearth, but is invisible to us because the inhabited part of Earth always faces away from it.)

sickle.

We also see that the ocean is disposed by the moon in accordance with hebdomadic numbers. It is visibly greatest during the flood-tide at the new moon, then on the second day it has withdrawn a bit, on the third day it is still less, and gradually the swelling of the flood-tide decreases more and more until the seventh day, which displays the moon halved, and then again, following this, on the eighth day it becomes again just as it was on the seventh day (that is, the same in power), and on the ninth as it was on the sixth, and on the tenth as it was on the fifth, and on the eleventh as it was on the fourth, and on the twelfth as it was on the third, and on the thirteenth as it was on the second, and on the fourteenth as it was on the first. And then, from a fresh beginning, the third hebdomad disposes the sphere of water in the same way as the first hebdomad did, and the fourth in the same way as the second.

What need is there now to go through the diminution of oysters and sea-urchins and mussels, and the sympathetic affection which most creatures undergo in relation to this heavenly body, when [61] we can derive sufficient proof of what is being said in the very things that happen to human beings? In the first place, women's evacuations occur by means of the aforementioned hebdomadic periods, and for this reason are called by some 'menses' and 'menstruation.'[18] Secondly, in general the male's seed is emitted seven times into the female's womb, and within seven hours at the most it either smears its fertile part for conception or slips away, just as, to be sure, at the opposite extreme, an interval of seven hours at least elapses between the natural severance of the baby's umbilical cord and its appearance and delivery, during which period the foetus is perfectly capable of surviving by itself, while it no longer behaves as if it were a plant or a part and is supported by nourishment from the umbilicus, nor yet does it behave like a living creature and is detached and self-sufficient thanks to breathing the outside air.

For seven days the embryo resembles a membranaceous, water-bearing kind of thing, as the physician Hippocrates agrees, when he

18. Both words are cognate with the word for 'month.'

says in *On the Nature of the Child*:[19]

> A female relative of mine had a particularly excellent and valu-
> able dancing-girl, who was going with a man, but did not want to
> get pregnant and be less highly prized by her admirers. The
> dancing-girl heard the sorts of things women say to one another,
> that when a woman is about to become pregnant the seed stays
> inside her and does not come out. She took in what she heard, and
> at one point she noticed that not [62] all the seed came out of her.
> She told her mistress, and word reached me. When I heard the
> news—it was on the seventh day—I instructed her to jump up
> high and to the ground. When she had done so seven times, the
> seed came out of her, accompanied by a noise. I will describe what
> the discharge was like: it was as if the surrounding shell of an egg
> had been stripped off, and within the internal membrane the
> moist part showed through.

That is from Hippocrates. And Strato the Peripatetic and Diocles
of Carystus and many other physicians say that during the second
hebdomad spots of blood appear on the membrane Hippocrates
mentioned, on the outside surface, and during the third they
penetrate through to the moist part, and during the fourth they say
that the moist part coagulates and the middle contains a node as if
of flesh and blood (obviously because it comes by completion due
to the perfect nature of 28, or because 28 contains the sum of the
two odd cubes, whose essence is limiting),[20] and during the fifth,
down to about the thirty-fifth day, the embryo is formed in the
middle of it, similar in size to a bee, but clearly articulated, so that
head and neck and trunk and limbs in general are apparent on it.
And they say that this embryo is viable in seven months, but if birth
is going to occur at nine months, then this formation happens in the
sixth hebdomad [63] for a female embryo, and in the seventh for a
male embryo.

That the hebdomad is particularly responsible for viability is
shown by the fact that even seven-month children are, thanks to it,

19. Chapter 13.

20. $28 = 1^3 + 3^3$. Cubes are said to be limiting because they encompass the limitation of solidity
and three-dimensionality.

no less likely to survive than nine-month ones, while eight-month children, which occur between both, perish from natural necessity. This fact the Pythagoreans, employing mathematical arguments and diagrams, used to deduce by means of considerations such as the following: they add together the basic cubes of the two smallest numbers—i.e. 8 and 27, the cubes of 2 and 3—to yield 35; in this number it turns out that the ratios of the concords, by means of which harmony is accomplished, are particularly evident.[21] For all generation is from opposites—moist and dry, cold and warm—and opposites do not concur nor do they come together into a compound of anything except under harmony. And the best of harmonies, which admits all the concordant ratios, is the one which falls under the number 35, which not only, as regards being made solid and complete, is accomplished by the two aforementioned cubes, which are equal-times-equal-times-equal, extended in three dimensions, but also is the combination of the first three perfect numbers, which are equal to their own parts—1 potentially, 6 and 28 actually.

Furthermore, it is also the summation of all the relationships of the concords which display in a basic way harmonic theory—6, 8, 9 and 12; and it has been shown earlier[22] that this 35, which is an enharmonic and particularly productive parallelogram encompassed by two odd sides 5 and 7 in length, is life-engendering, if extended and raised to a third dimension by 6 (for 6 is most suited to soul, the life-force).

Quality [64] and color and light accompany corporeal magnitudes in three dimensions and evidently fall under the pentad;[23] ensoulment and the condition of life fall under the hexad, which is why it is so called;[24] completion and thought fall under the hebdomad. The product of 5x6x7 or 7x6x5 would obviously also be the result of 5x7x6: all of them are 210, which is the number of days in which seven-month children are engendered, apart from the six

21. See also pp. 78, 83.
22. See p. 83.
23. See pp. 66, 73, 103.
24. See p. 77, n. 7.

days during which the compound, the moisture-bearing membrane, was shown first to appear; but if these six are brought in, the result would be the recurrent and spherical cube of the soul's number six, which is made equal to its own parts.

Diocles says that when 35 is multiplied by 6, the resulting 210 is a solid number, because 210 is the number of days in seven months of thirty days. And Hippocrates says: "What moves in 70 days is accomplished in triple the number."[25] For in fact according to him it is the trebling of 70 days that makes 210, and of 90 that makes 270—the periods of seven-month and nine-month children.

All seeds appear above ground, during growth, in the course of the seventh day or thereabouts, and the majority of them are seven-stemmed for the most part. Just as foetuses were sown and ordered in the womb by the hebdomad, so also after birth in seven hours they reach the crisis of whether or not they will live. For all those which are born complete and not dead come out of the womb breathing, [65] but as regards the acceptance of the air which is being breathed and by which soul in general acquires tension, they are confirmed at the critical seventh hour one way or the other—either towards life or towards death.

Children cut their teeth at seven months, and at twice seven sit up and gain an unswaying posture, and at three times seven they begin to articulate speech and make their first efforts at talking, and at four times seven they stand without falling over and try to walk, and at five times seven they are naturally weaned and milk ceases to be their food. And at seven years they shed their natural teeth and grow ones which are suitable for hard food, and at twice seven years they come to puberty and, just as in the first hebdomad of years they acquired in an articulated manner the full range of *expressed* speech, consisting of as many simple words as are natural and useful for such expression, so they now begin to embark on the articulation of *abstract* speech, in so far as there is now a rational creature, and there being, according to most philosophers, seven senses which train the rational and are completed especially at this

25. *Epidemics* III.453 (Kühn).

time: for in addition to the commonly recognized five senses, some count the faculties of speech and procreation, and the latter is completed at the time when the procreative faculty [66] naturally changes for all humans—for males by means of seed, for females by means of menstruation. Hence they only then acquire fitness for engendering life, and among the Babylonians they do not play a part in religious ceremonies or partake in their priestly wisdom, but are debarred from all the initiations there before this time.

Since in the next period[26] it is possible for them to have children and substitute others for themselves for the fulfillment of the universe, then the poets are being reasonable when they classify a generation as the thirty-year symmetry of the appearance of children; and because of the perfection of the triad, a complete succession consists of three—father, son and grandson.

In the third hebdomad, they generally conclude growth in terms of length, and in the fourth they complete growth in terms of breadth, and there is no other bodily increase remaining to them; for 28 is a complete number.

In the fifth hebdomad, thanks to the manifestation of the harmonic 35, all increase as regards strength is checked, and after these years it is no longer possible for people to become stronger than they are. Hence, when athletes reach this age, some have already stopped winning and do not expect to achieve anything more, though others do not yet give up. And the legal codes of the best constitutions have conscription up to this hebdomad (though some have it until the next hebdomad), and after this point allow people to be officers, but not to serve in the ranks any more.

Finally, when the principle of the decad is blended with that of the hebdomad and ten times seven is reached, then man should be released from all tasks [67] and dedicated to the enjoyment of happiness, as they say.

If there are four elements, and there are necessarily three means between them, then here too a hebdomad will control all things. This is obviously why Linus the theologian, in the second book on

26. That is, in the period 21-28, since the previous paragraph discussed 14-21.

theology of his *To Hymenaeus*, says: "The four sources of every-thing are controlled by triple bonds." For fire and earth are linked to each other by geometrical proportion: as earth is to air, so water is to fire, and conversely as fire is to air, so water is to earth, and vice versa.[27] The harmonies of such things are in a sense unifying, and between air and fire there is persuasion: for the elements from air to earth are assimilated to the heavenly bodies by desire and imitation, and always remain in the same condition, being in a sense persuaded and guided by the nature of the primordial beauty which attracts everything to itself.

Moreover, the hebdomad has the property of being the most critical number, not only in pregnancy and in the ages of life development, but also in disease and health, because it is the most akin and cognate to the human constitution: for our so-called black internal organs are seven and fall under it (they are tongue, heart, liver, lung, spleen and two kidneys), and [68] there are this many parts of the body in general (i.e. head, trunk, two arms, two legs, and genitals). And taken part by part, there are 7 channels in the face—2 for eyes, 2 for ears, 2 for nostrils and one for mouth—and 7 which transmit breath and food—throat, gullet, stomach, guts, intestinal membrane, bladder and the one by the seat, which some call rectum.

It is possible to live for 7 days with no intake of food. And in geometrical research there are seven types of source which they have identified—point, line, surface, angle, shape, solid and plane; and seven is the quota of the most elementary to admit investiga-tion: for a triangle has three angles, an equal number of sides, and its area is single.

Furthermore, symptoms are confirmed by means of the hebdo-mad, as inclining either towards sickness or towards health: for all types of fever meet at the seventh day and at no other before it, and so they reach crisis at this point. This can be simply and plausibly

27. See Plato, *Timaeus* 32b.

demonstrated by means of the property of the various proportionate series from the monad which we set out earlier, when we saw that the first and seventh places alone admit both cubes and squares, the fifth and third admit only squares, the fourth admits only cubes, and the second and sixth admit neither, just as among the types of fever they admit neither the tertian nor the quartan.[28]

For 1, 3, 5 and 7 participate in what is called tertian fever, since it is particularly like a square because [69] a square has its origin in plane triangles whose equality of right angles and sides the perfectly commensurate square contains, and is made regular in relation to itself,[29] and since its symptoms always become apparent with a day's interval in between; so these numbers participate in it because they are at a third remove from one another,[30] just as they participate in squaring in all the proportionate series by being evenly distributed through the places.

And 1, 4 and 7 participate in quartan fever, which is attended by cubes because it is altogether stable and steadfast as a result of the six square bases. For the process manifests symptoms with two days' interval in between, and consequently occurs on the fourth day, as in the proportionate series cubes are always accomplished at the fourth place.

The so-called semi-tertian fever does not have a nature peculiar to itself, but is formed by the tertian. It occurs within two periods of a night and a day each (i.e. within 48 hours), but it always cuts off three hours, as it reaches one of the two possibilities—attack or remission of the fever—and then passes to the opposite for one twelve-hour period. (It can, however, yield its symptoms earlier or later; depending on what it does, it is called great semi-tertian or small or median, with regard to the delays of or extensions to either possibility.) The second twelve-hour period of the second day will participate in the fever, as will the first twelve-hour period of the

28. See p. 62 with n. 22, and p. 87.

29. The Greek is very obscure and has required emendation to get even this far. There seems to be a reference to the Platonic composition of squares out of two equal right-angled isosceles triangles; hence tertian fever is like a square because both it and triangles are three-fold.

30. The Greeks counted inclusively and hence, for instance, described as 'the third day away' what we would call 'the day after tomorrow.'

fourth and the beginning of the sixth: these are the periods during which the symptoms become clear. The result is that there is again an onset of the fever in the later period of the seventh day.[31]

In a sense the seventh day is in all respects like the first: for these two days are the only ones which partake of all the types of fever up to and including the quartan interval, and the first day will be generative, so to speak, [70] of fevers, while the seventh will be critical and, as it were, testing; but none of all the days in between partakes of all the types—except that they all partake of quotidian fever, as necessarily the seventh and the first do too, since this is the only shared manifestation of symptoms, as the displayed diagrams show.[32]

This multiplicity is an attribute common to all series, but the second place in the series escapes tertian and quartan fevers, but partakes of quotidian and semi-tertian; the third place escapes semi-tertian and quartan, but partakes of quotidian and tertian; the fourth place escapes tertian, but partakes of the three remaining types of fever; the fifth place escapes quartan, but partakes of tertian and quotidian and the irregularity of the remaining one; the sixth, contrary to the fourth, which escaped only one, partakes only of the quotidian; the seventh partakes of them all, as does the first.[33]

Since the features of the other types are more obvious or simple, but the semi-tertian is disorderly, then it should be defined more clearly, as follows: the symptoms will not become clear within five six-hour periods from the initial source of the symptoms; this

31. We can encapsulate this paragraph in the following diagram, where the numbers are hours and the peaks are the points at which the symptoms become clear (i.e. the crisis points):

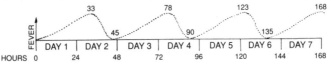

32. Presumably the text was originally accompanied by linear diagrams, divided into days and marking the occurrences of the various types of disease.

33. In this paragraph it is denied that the semi-tertian occurs on the third or sixth days. However, in both the earlier and later paragraphs on the semi-tertian, both of these days are mentioned. It may well be that this whole paragraph is a later interpolation by an editor (or even our compiler) trying, unsuccessfully, to explain the diagrams which originally accompanied the text: for not only does this paragraph contradict the surrounding material in our treatise, but it

means that, if the previous manifestation of symptoms occurred at noon of the second day, it will be on the evening of the third day that the following manifestation will have its *terminus post quem*, while moreover midnight on the fourth day will go up to the very early morning of the sixth, and the result is that there is a crisis at noon on the seventh. This distribution is that of the smallest semitertian and can be used as a basis to calculate the irregularities.[34]

Since everything comes together and is distinguished by coincidence and in a critical manner at the place of the hebdomad, they called it 'critical time' and 'Chance,' and [71] custom has entrenched the habit of saying 'critical time and Chance' together. Why need people now quibble about the hebdomadic critical points which astrologers in particular believe in?

They called the heptad 'Athena' and 'critical time' and 'Chance'—'Athena' because it is a virgin and unwed, just like Athena in myth,[35] and is born neither of mother (i.e. of even number) nor of father (i.e. odd number), but from the head of the father of all (i.e. from the monad, the head of number); and like Athena it is not womanish, but divisible number is female. They called it 'critical time' because it encompasses, in a short span of time, activities when they are in crisis and are tending to health or sickness, or to generation or destruction. They called it 'Chance' because, just like Chance in myth, it controls mortal affairs.

There are 7 elementary sounds not only for human speech, [36] but also for the sounds which instruments and the universe make—in short, for enharmonic sound—not only because of the single, primary sounds emitted by the 7 heavenly bodies, as we learn, but also because the prime diagram among musicians has turned out to be the heptachord.

*

also contradicts the whole Greek medical tradition's descriptions of the semi-tertian, whereas the other two paragraphs of our treatise do not.

34. Noon on the second day is the thirty-sixth hour of the total stretch: the four possible thirty-hour intervals fall where this paragraph says they do.

35. See p. 90.

36. The seven vowels of the Greek alphabet.

While there are three kinds or parts of the soul (rational, spirited and appetitive), there are four complete virtues,[37] just as while there are three dimensions, there are four limits in corporeal increase.[38]

37. Wisdom, justice, courage and moderation; see p. 59.
38. The four points of the pyramid, the basic three-dimensional body.

On the Octad

[72] We describe the octad as the first actual cube, and as the only number within the decad to be even-times-even, since 4 appears to combine the characteristics of being odd-even and even-times-even in admitting only two divisions up to the monad, one of itself, the other of its parts.[1]

All the ways in which it is put together are excellent and equilibrated tunings. First, it results from the only two numbers within the decad which are neither engenderers nor engendered (I mean, from 1 and 7); then, it results from the two which are even-odd, one potentially, the other actually—i.e. from 2 and 6; then, it results from the first two odd numbers—i.e. from 3 and 5 (and this is the combination which is elementary for the generation of cubes, and is the first such sum, since the cube before it, 1, comes about without combination, while the one after it results from the next three odd numbers—7, 9 and 11—and the one after *that* from 4 continuous odd numbers—13, 15, 17 and 19);[2] and fourthly, it results from 4 taken twice, and four is the only number which both engenders [73] and is engendered.[3] The consequence is that 8 is completed by means of the first two unengendered numbers, and from their opposites (numbers which engender) and from the number which contains both characteristics. (Moreover, we have shown that 4 is the dividing line of harmonic relations—the dividing line between the concords within it, and the melodies,

---

1. Insofar as 2 is both even and odd, then 4 is both odd-even and even-times-even. The author (probably Nicomachus here) refers to the "two divisions up to the monad" simply to emphasize that 2 is the chief factor of 4. As a matter of fact, however, 4 was usually a standard even-times-even number.

2. And so on: see Glossary under *Cube*.

3. Four is the only number within the decad which both engenders another number within the decad (2x4=8) *and* is engendered by another number (2x2=4).

which are not actual concords, after it.)⁴ Hence they used to call the ogdoad 'embracer of all harmonies' because of this marvellous attunement, or because it is the first to have been attuned and multiplied so as to be equal-times-equal-times-equal, which is a most lawful generation. So when they call it 'Cadmean,' they should be understood to be referring to the fact that, as all historians tell us, Harmonia was the wife of Cadmus.

Clear traces of the ogdoad can be found in the heavens too: for there are eight spheres of the heavenly bodies, and there are eight circles which astronomers most need to understand and which are most useful for knowledge. The four greatest of these are the ones which touch one another (in a sense at two points, but in a sense otherwise)⁵—the equator, the zodiac, the horizon, and the one which passes through the poles, which some call the meridian, others the colure; the four lesser ones, which do not touch one another at all, are the Arctic and Antarctic circles and the summer and winter tropics.

Moreover, there are similar features among the things of the Earth, since the ogdoad contains the limit for creatures which have feet, and after it there is indeterminacy: there are scorpions and crabs and similar creatures among those which have a definite number of feet, but any subsequent creatures [74] are among those which are simply many-footed.

The four-fold distribution of the teeth of human beings is in a way ogdoadic⁶ and the distinction of the four apertures of the head is defined by the ogdoad;⁷ and there are analogously similar aspects to creatures' teats and claws.⁸

4. The closest we get to this in our treatise is p. 63, where all the harmonic ratios were shown to reside in the first four numbers. The melodic ratios, however, are the semitone (16:15 or 256:243), the major tone (9:8), the minor tone (10:9), the major third (5:4) and the minor third (6:5).

5. I suppose this is a compressed way of saying that they do not all touch one another at the same two points.

6. Counting from the middle of the mouth, there are eight teeth in each quadrant (thirty-two in all).

7. Perhaps because we have two ears, two eyes, two nostrils and channels for both food and air through the mouth.

8. Presumably he is referring to those animals which have eight teats, and to birds, which have four claws on each foot.

Hence they used to call the ogdoad 'mother,' perhaps referring to what has already been said (for even number is female), but perhaps, since Rhea is the mother of the gods, because although the dyad was shown to belong to Rhea seminally, the ogdoad does in extension.[9] And some think that they very word 'ogdoad' was coined to resemble 'ekdyad'—that is, the one which is generated 'out of the dyad,' when it is cubed.

Philolaus says that after mathematical magnitude has become three-dimensional thanks to the tetrad, there is the quality and 'color' of visible Nature in the pentad, and ensoulment in the hexad, and intelligence and health and what he calls 'light' in the hebdomad, and then next, with the ogdoad, things come by love and friendship and wisdom and creative thought.

The ogdoad is 'untimely for birth.' In the case of Rhea, the myths tell us that Kronos (as the stories go) disposed of her children; and in the case of the ogdoad, labor in the eighth month is fruitless and hence is called 'untimely.'

Among the number of the Muses, they said that the name 'Euterpe' was suitable for the ogdoad, because it is the most changeable of the numbers within the decad, since it is even-times-even and is divisible up to the monad itself, which is naturally indivisible.[10]

From Anatolius

[75] The ogdoad is called 'safety' and 'foundation,' since it is a leader, because two is a leader:[11] the seed of the ogdoad is the first even number. When multiplied by the tetrad it makes 32, which is the time in which they say that seven-month children are formed.[12]

The eighth sphere encompasses the whole—hence the saying 'All is eight.' "In eight spheres they revolve in a circle around the

9. See p. 46: 8 is 2^3.

10. Euterpe, the 'well-pleasing' Muse, is associated with *eutreptos* (changeable).

11. Perhaps the meaning of this condensed sentence is that 2 is a leader because it is a source of number; 8 is 2^3, i.e. made solid and stable; so 8 is a stable leader.

12. Compare p. 92.

ninth, Earth," says Eratosthenes.[13]

The number 8 is the source of the musical ratios, and the terms of the composition of the universe are as follows: the number 8 is in a sesquioctaval relation to 9 (9 exceeds 8 by a monad); 12 is the sequialter of 8 and the sesquitertian of 9 (it exceeds 9 by a triad); 16 is the sesquitertian of 12 (the excess is 4); 18 is the sesquialter of 12 (the excess is a hexad); 21 is the double sesquitertian of 9 (the excess is 12); 24 is the sesquitertian of 18 (the excess is 6); 32 is the sesquitertian of 24 (the excess is 8); 36 is double 18 and the sesquialter of 24 (the excess is 12).

The 9 of the moon is in sesquioctaval relation to 8; the 12 of Mercury is the sesquialter of 8; the 16 of Venus is double 8; the 18 of the sun is double 9 and the sesquioctave of 16; the 21 of Mars is the double sesquitertian of 9; the 24 of Jupiter is double 12, which is the sesquialter of 8; the 32 of Saturn is quadruple 8; the 36 of the fixed stars is quadruple 9 and [76] the sesquioctave of 32.

The excesses are: 36, by 4; 32, by 8; 24, by 3; 21, by 3; 18, by 2; 16, by 4; 12, by 3; 9, by 1. Alternatively, 9 exceeds 8 by a monad, 12 exceeds 9 by a triad, 16 exceeds 12 by a tetrad, 18 exceeds 16 by a dyad, and so on for the rest.

13. Fragment 17 (Hiller).

On the Ennead

The ennead is the greatest of the numbers within the decad and is an unsurpassable limit. At any rate, it marks the end of the formation of specific identities as follows: not only does it happen that, after the ninth pitch, there is no further superparticular musical ratio,[1] but also addition naturally turns from the natural end to the beginning,[2] and (as was shown in more detail in the diagrammatic representation of justice in relation to the pentad)[3] from both of these to the middle. At any rate, as regards the word, it is probably a riddling reference to affinity and equivalence, in the sense that it is called 'ennead' as if it were the 'henad'[4] of everything within it, by derivation from 'one.'

That number admits nothing beyond the ennead, but rather everything circles around within it, is clear from the so-called recurrences: there is natural progression up to it, but after it there is repetition. For 10 becomes a monad by the subtraction of one elementary quantity (i.e. one ennead), and again 11 and 20 become a dyad by the subtraction of either one or two enneads, and 12 and 30 become a triad, [77] and again 100 becomes a monad, when 11 enneads are subtracted, and so on *ad infinitum*, so that it is by no means possible for there to subsist any number beyond the nine elementary numbers.[5] Hence they called it 'Oceanus'[6] and 'horizon,' because it encompasses both of these locations and has them within itself.[7]

---

1. See p. 79, n. 14 on superparticulars. The 'musical ratios' are the octave (2:1), the fourth (4:3), the fifth (3:2), the third (5:4), and the tone (9:8); so 9 is the largest number to appear in them.

2. See the next paragraph.

3. See pp. 68-72.

4. Another word for monad: *hen* is 'one.'

5. See also p. 77, n. 6.

6. Oceanus was envisaged as an expanse of water encircling the outer limits of the world.

7. Because all things are made from number and 9 is the furthest limit of number.

Other evidence led them to call it 'Prometheus,' because it prevents any number from proceeding further than itself,[8] as is reasonable, since it is thrice perfect[9] and does not lack the advantage of multiplication, but in fact is both the combination of two cubes (1 and 8) and, since it is a square, it alone of the numbers up to it has a triangular number as its square root.

At any rate, because it does not allow the harmony of number to be dissipated beyond itself, but brings numbers together and makes them play in concert, it is called 'concord' and 'limitation,' and also 'sun,' in the sense that it gathers things together.[10]

It is called 'lack of strife' because of the correspondence and interchange of numbers from it to the monad, as was discussed in the diagram about justice.[11]

It was called 'assimilation,' perhaps because it is the first odd square (for odd numbers are called 'assimilative' in general because of assimilation; and moreover, squares are assimilative, oblongs are dissimilar), [12] and perhaps also because it is particularly assimilated to its square root: for just as that has obtained the third place in the natural progression, so also the ennead is third in the corresponding progression by threes.[13]

They used to call it 'Hephaestus,' because the way up to it is, as it were, [78] by smelting and evaporation;[14] and 'Hera' because the sphere of air falls under it, since this sphere is the ninth over the other eight;[15] and 'sister-consort of Zeus' because of its being paired with the monad;[16] and 'banisher' because it prevents the voluntary

8. See the supposed etymology of 'Prometheus' at p. 38, n. 10.

9. Because 3 is a perfect number.

10. *Halios* (sun) is linked with *halizein* (gather together).

11. See pp. 68-72, on the pentad, which is also called 'lack of strife' (p. 68).

12. Squares are the products of equal, i.e. similar, factors; and the sequence of odd numbers forms squares (see Glossary under *Gnomon*).

13. That is, the triple sequence of 1, 3, 9, 27, etc.

14. Hephaestus was the metallurgical god; perhaps the image is supposed to suggest that 'smelting' is the fusion of monads into the sequence of numbers, but the monad is not exhausted—some part of it 'evaporates,' in the sense that it can continue the sequence.

15. The name Hera is linked with *aer* (air). A common Greek model saw the universe as concentric spheres of the elements, from the most dense at the middle to the most refined at the outside (see also the mention of the 'sphere of water' on p. 91, and pp. 40, 68).

16. That is, as the beginning and end of the natural sequence of numbers. Hera was Zeus' sister and wife.

progress of number;[17] and 'finishing-post' because it has been organized as the goal and, as it were, turning-point of advancement.[18]

Both Orpheus and Pythagoras made a particular point of describing the ennead as 'pertaining to the Curetes,' on the grounds that the rites sacred to the Curetes are tripartite,[19] with three rites in each part, or as 'Kore':[20] both of these titles are appropriate to the triad, and the ennead contains the triad three times. They also called it 'Hyperion,' because it has gone beyond all the other numbers as regards magnitude,[21] and 'Terpsichore,' because the recurrence of the principles and their convergence on it as if from an end to a mid-point and to the beginning is like the turning and revolution of a dance.[22]

The ennead is the first square based on an odd number. It too is called 'that which brings completion,' and it completes nine-month children;[23] moreover, it is called 'perfect,' because it arises out of 3, which is a perfect number. The heavenly spheres revolve around the Earth, which is ninth. Nine is also said [79] to contain the principles of the concords—4, 3 and 2: the sesquitertian is 4:3, the sesquialter is 3:2, and the double is 4:2. It is the first number to be in the sesquioctaval ratio.

17. Apollo's title of *hekaergos* (banisher) is derived here from *eirgein* (prevent) and *hekas* (voluntary).

18. See p. 77, n. 6.

19. The Curetes were Cretan deities who in myth looked after the infant Zeus.

20. Persephone.

21. Hyperion was a Titan; strictly, he was the father of the sun, but he was often equated with the sun; the word 'Hyperion' could mean 'going beyond.'

22. Terpsichore, one of the Muses, is assimilated to *trepein* (to turn) and *chorus* (dance); in fact, her name means 'delighter in dance.'

23. Compare p. 87 on the hebdomad.

On the Decad

We have often said before[1] that the creative mind wrought the construction and composition of the universe and everything in the universe by reference to the likeness and similarity of number, as if to a perfect paradigm. But since the whole was an indefinite multitude and the whole substance of number was inexhaustible, it was not reasonable or scientific to employ an incomprehensible paradigm, and there was a need of commensurability, so that the Creator God, in his craftsmanship, might prevail over and overcome the terms and measures which were set before him, and might neither contract in an inferior fashion nor expand in a discordant fashion to a lesser or greater result than what was appropriate. However, a natural equilibration and commensurability and wholeness existed above all in the decad. It has encompassed seminally within itself all things, both solid and plane, even and odd and even-odd, perfect in all manners of perfection, prime and incomposite, and equality and inequality, the ten relations,[2] and diagonal numbers, spherical numbers and circular numbers; in itself it has no special or natural variation, apart from the fact that it runs and circles back to itself.[3] Hence it was reasonable for God to use it as a measure for things and as a gnomon and straight edge when he added things to one another and fitted them together harmoniously. And this is why, both in general and in particular, things from heaven to Earth [80] are found to have been organized by it.

Hence the Pythagoreans in their theology called it sometimes 'universe,' sometimes 'heaven,' sometimes 'all,' sometimes 'Fate'

---

1. Not in our treatise; this is another excerpt from Nicomachus' *Theology of Arithmetic.*

2. Either the ten proportions of Greek mathematics, or the ten modes of inequality (see p. 79, n. 14).

3. See p. 77, n. 6.

and 'eternity,' 'power' and 'trust' and 'Necessity,' 'Atlas' and 'unwearying,' and simply 'God' and 'Phanes'[4] and 'sun.'

They called it 'universe,' because all things are arranged by it both in general and in particular;[5] and because it is the most perfect boundary of number, in the sense that 'decad' is, as it were, 'receptacle,'[6] just as heaven is the receptacle of all things, they called it 'heaven' and, among the Muses, 'Ourania.'[7]

They called it 'all' because there is no natural number greater than it, but, if one thinks about it, number recurs and circles back, in a sense, to the decad; for a hekatontad is ten decads, and a chiliad is ten hekatontads, and a myriad is ten chiliads, and similarly any other number recurs and retrogresses either to the decad or to some number within the decad. Anyway, the reduction and returning of all numbers to it is manifold.

Alternatively, the decad is called 'all' because of the mythical Pan;[8] for Pan is honored by means of the decad (that is, he is honored on the tenth day of the month) and he is honored by ten (that is, generally speaking, by shepherds, goatherds, cowherds, horse-keepers, soldiers, hunters, sailors, gardeners, woodcutters and those [81] who lay foundations). And it is said that ten species of animals live with the human race—dog, bird, cow, horse, ass, mule, goose, goat, sheep and ferret.

Again, they called it 'Fate,' because there is no attribute, either among numbers or among things which have been formed by numbers, which is not sown in the decad and the numbers within it, and does not also extend, in the remaining series, step by step, to what follows the decad; and Fate is as it were a connected and orderly result.[9]

It is called 'eternity' because eternity, which encompasses all things, is said, since it is complete and everlasting, to bring everything to fulfillment, like the decad.

4. The name of the Creator in Orphic cosmogony.
5. *Kosmos* (universe) means literally 'order' or 'arrangement.'
6. *Dechas*, a word coined by Pythagoreans for this purpose.
7. Her name is cognate with the word for 'heaven.'
8. His name means 'all.'
9. *Heimarmene* (Fate) is here related to *heirmos* (series).

It is called 'power,' because the things of the universe are strengthened by it, and ten appears to control the other numbers and all principles as a defence and enclosure and receptacle; hence it was also called 'custodian,' because it is a compound of the numbers up to and including the tetrad.[10]

Moreover, it is called 'trust' because, according to Philolaus, it is thanks to the decad and its parts that we have secure trust in things being precisely comprehensible. And this is why it might also be called 'memory,' for the same reasons that the monad was called 'memory.'[11]

Given that theologians claim in unison that Necessity occupies the most remote rim of the whole heaven, and perpetually drives and urges on the whole rotation with an adamantine and indefatigable whip,[12] then [82] the decad would be 'Necessity,' since it circumscribes everything and, by mingling things one with another and again separating them, it imbues things with change and continuity.

The spheres of the universe are ten and fall under the decad.[13] It is called 'Atlas' because in myth the Titan carries heaven on his shoulders (as Homer says: "He holds the great pillars which keep Earth and heaven apart")[14] and the decad holds together the principles of the spheres, as if it were a diameter of all of them, which both turns them around and limits them, so that they can be best maintained.[15]

Speusippus, the son of Plato's sister Potone, and head of the Academy before Xenocrates, compiled a polished little book from the Pythagorean writings which were particularly valued at any time, and especially from the writings of Philolaus; he entitled the book *On Pythagorean Numbers*. In the first half of the book, he

10. The tetrad is also the 'custodian': see p. 62.
11. The monad is not called 'memory' in our treatise, but it is said to be the source of all knowledge (p. 37).
12. cf. Plato, *Republic* 616c.
13. See p. 90, n. 17.
14. *Odyssey* I. 53-4.
15. Compare Plato's image of Necessity as a spindle running through the spheres of the universe (*Republic* 616c).

elegantly expounds linear numbers, polygonal numbers and all sorts of plane numbers, solid numbers and the five figures which are assigned to the elements of the universe, discussing both their individual attributes and their shared features, and their proportionality and reciprocity. Next, in the remaining half of the book, [83] he goes straight on to deal with the decad, which he shows to be the most natural and fulfilling of things, because it is (in itself, and not by our contrivance or by chance) the kind of thing which creates the finished products of the universe, and is a foundation-stone and was set before God who created the universe as a completely perfect paradigm. He speaks in this manner about the decad:[16]

> Ten is a perfect number, and it is both correct and in accordance with Nature that we Greeks and all men, without making any special effort, arrive at this number in all sorts of ways when we count. For it has many of the properties which are suitable for a number that is perfect in this way, and it also has many properties which are not peculiar to it, but which a perfect number ought to have.
>
> So, in the first place, a perfect number ought to be even, so that it contains an equal amount of odd and even numbers, without imbalance; for since an odd number always precedes an even number, then if the final number is not even, the other sort will predominate.
>
> Secondly, it is necessary for a perfect number to contain an equal amount of prime and incomposite numbers, and secondary and composite numbers.[17] Ten does have an equal amount, and no number less than ten has this property, though numbers more that ten might (such as twelve and others),[18] but ten is the base number of the series. Since it is the first and smallest of those numbers which have this property, it has a kind of perfection, and this is a property peculiar to it, that [84] it is the first in which an equal amount of incomposite and composite numbers are seen.

16. Speusippus, fragment 4 (Lang), fragment 28 (Tarán).

17. Speusippus, therefore, counts 2 as prime (see Glossary under *Prime*): 1, 2, 3, 5, and 7 are prime; 4, 6, 8, 9 and 10 are secondary.

18. Only 12 and 14, in fact.

Moreover, in addition to this property, it contains an equal amount of multiples and submultiples: for it contains as submultiples all the numbers up to and including five, while those from six to ten are multiples of the former ones. But since seven is a multiple of none of them, it must be excluded, and so must four, as a multiple of two, with the result that the amounts are again equal.[19]

Furthermore, all the ratios are contained by 10—that of the equal, and the greater and the less, and the superparticular and all the remaining kinds are in it, as are linear, plane and solid numbers. For one is a point, two a line, three a triangle and four a pyramid: these are all primary and are the sources of the things which are of the same category as each of them. In these numbers is also seen the first of the proportions, which is the one where the ratios of excess are constant and the limit is ten.[20]

The primary elements in plane and solid figures are these: point, line, triangle, pyramid. They contain the number ten and are limited by it. For there is a tetrad in the angles or bases of a pyramid, and a hexad in its sides, which makes 10. And again, there is a tetrad in the intervals and limits of a point and a line, and a hexad in the sides and angles of a triangle, which again makes 10.[21]

Moreover, if one looks [85] at figures in terms of number, there is the same result.[22] The first triangle is the equilateral, which has in a sense a single line and angle—I say it is single, because its sides and angles are equal, and what is equal is always indivisible

19. Speusippus wants all the numbers from 1 to 5 to be submultiples, and all those from 6 to 10 to be multiples, but 4 and 7 are in the wrong halves of the decad for this, since 4 is not prime, but is a multiple, and 7 is prime.

20. That is, 1, 2, 3, 4, which add up to 10.

21. Take a triangle: it has three sides and three angles, totalling 6. So far, so good: the problem is to see how he is getting a tetrad out of the "intervals and limits of a point and a line." Perhaps it is as follows: the apexes of the triangle are three points A, B, and C. The base line BC has two limits (the point B and C), and the final point A is related by an interval twice to this base line— once to B and once to C.

22. The rest of this fragment of Speusippus is usually dismissed by commentators as worthless rubbish, but what he says is remarkably similar to the modern mathematical concept of 'degrees of freedom.' An equilateral triangle is said to have only one degree of freedom, because you have to specify only one thing—the length of the side(s)—to define it; an isosceles triangle has two degrees of freedom, because you have to specify two things to define it—the length of the two equal sides, and the length of the other side; and so on.

and uniform. The second triangle is the the half-square, which has
a single distinction of lines and angles, and so is seen is terms of
the dyad. The third is the half-triangle (i.e. half an equilateral
triangle): it is altogether unequal in each respect, so from all
points of view its number is three. And you would find the same
sort of thing in the case of solid figures, but going up to four, so that
in this way too you come across a decad.[23]

For in a sense the first pyramid, which is based on an equilateral
triangle, has a single—because equal—line and face; and the
second, which is erected on a square, is two, because of the single
distinction it has by being bounded by three planes at the angle on
the base, but being enclosed by four at the apex, so that as a result
of this it is like the dyad; the third, which is set on a half-square,
is informed by a triad, and along with the single distinction we
have already observed in the half-square as a plane figure, it has
another difference too, in having an angle at the apex, which
results in this pyramid (the one in which the angle at the apex is
perpendicular to the middle of the side of the base) being assimilated to the triad; and the fourth, which is based on a half-triangle,
is for similar reasons informed by a tetrad. The result is that the
limit of the mentioned figures is ten. And the same things occur
also in generating such figures: for the first source where magnitude is concerned is the point, the second is the line, the third is
surface and the fourth is solid.

From Anatolius

[86] The decad is potentially generated by even and odd: for 10 is
five times two. It is the perimeter and limit of all number: for they
run their course by wheeling and turning around it as if it were a
turning-point in a race.[24] Moreover, it is the limit of the infinitude
of numbers.

It is called 'power' and 'all-fulfiller,' because it limits all number
by encompassing within itself the whole nature of even and odd,

---

23. As he says at the end of the fragment, he is talking here about the *limits* of point, line,
triangle and pyramid. The limit of a point is 1, the limit of a line is 2—these are obvious and are
not discussed. The limits of (the most distinctions within) any sort of triangle is 3 (argued for
in this paragraph); the limit in the same way of any sort of pyramid is 4 (argued for in the next
paragraph). So again we have the decad of 1, 2, 3, 4.

24. See p. 77, n. 6.

moving and unmoving, good and bad. Moreover, it arises out of the tetraktys of the first numbers (1, 2, 3 and 4) combined; and 20 arises out of twice of each of them.

Moreover, the decad generates the number 55,[25] which encompasses wonderful beauties. For in the first place, this is formed by doubling and trebling the systematic sequence of numbers—the doubles are 1, 2, 4, 8 (i.e. 15), the triples are 1, 3, 9, 27 (i.e. 40), and the addition of these makes 55. Plato also mentions these sequences in the passage on the generation of soul which begins, "He removed one portion from the whole," and so on.[26]

In the second place, while 55 is a construct of the decad, 385 is an addition of the squared decad: for if you square the successive numbers from the monad to the decad, and then add them up, you will get the aforementioned number, 385; and this is also 7x55.

Moreover, if you count the letters of the word 'one,' you will find by addition 55.[27]

Moreover, if the hexad, the most fertile number, is squared, [87] it produces 36, and this has seven factors, generated as follows: 18 taken twice, 12 taken three times, 9 taken four times, 6 taken six times, 4 taken nine times, 3 taken twelve times, and 2 taken eighteen times. These seven factors, and the number itself, make 55.[28]

Moreover, the sequence of the first five triangular numbers generates 55 (3, 6, 10, 15 and 21 make 55) and again, the sequence of the first five squares generates 55 (1, 4, 9, 16 and 25 make 55); and according to Plato the universe is generated out of triangle and square.[29] For he constructs three figures out of equilateral triangles—pyramid, octahedron and icosahedron, which are the figures respectively of fire, air and water—and the cube, the figure of earth, out of squares.[30]

25. 1+2 . . . +10=55.
26. *Timaeus* 35b; see also p. 29.
27. See p. 39, n. 15: *hen* (one) adds up to 55.
28. That is, adding the factors (2, 3, 4, 6, 9, 12 and 18) to the monad (1 itself, taken once), makes 55.
29. *Timaeus* 53c-56c.
30. Pythagoreans were doubtless aware also that $3025=55^2=(1+2+3 \ldots +10)^2=1^3+2^3+3^3 \ldots +10^3$. Equally doubtless, they would have been delighted to know that 55 is the tenth number in the Fibonacci series!

Glossary

It is impossible, of course, to know in advance which of the many technical terms that appear in our treatise will not be familiar to readers. This glossary contains only the most outlandish and/or most peculiarly Greek mathematical terminology. Any gaps can be filled, and further information provided, by works mentioned in the Bibliography.

A. Types of Number

Circular: A square number whose last digit is the same as the last digit of the side number (root); so a circular number is bound to end in 1, 5 or 6. Examples: 25 (5²), 1296 (36²).

Composite: see *Secondary*.

Cube: A number which can be portrayed as a cubical array of evenly spaced dots. These are the familiar cubes. Also called 'equal-times-equal-times-equal.' Note that the first cube is the sum of the first odd number (1); the second cube is the sum of the next two odd numbers (3, 5); the third cube of the next three, and so on. See also: *Spherical.*

Defective: A number which is greater than the sum of its factors. Example: 8, whose factors (1, 2, 4) add up to 7.

Diagonal: A number considered as the diagonal of a square. See also under *Side.*

Even: A number which can be divided into two equal parts *and* into two unequal parts. Hence 2, which can be divided only into two equal parts, is a source of number, rather than an actual number.

Even-odd: A number which is even, but whose half is odd. There is also a loose sense of the term, in which it means 'both even and odd at once.'

Even-times-even: To earlier Greek mathematicians, this was any number which is the product of two even numbers. To later mathematicians, it is a number which can be successively halved down to 1. Example: 16, halved to 8, 4, 2, 1.

Imperfect: See *Defective.*

Incomposite: See *Prime.*

Linear: A number represented as a straight line of dots. Thus any number *can* be linear, but only prime numbers are exclusively linear, since they cannot be plane or solid numbers.

Mixed: A secondary number which shares with some other secondary number no factor except for 1. Example: 9 and 25 are mixed in relation to each other, since their factors (3 and 5 respectively) do not overlap.

Oblong: A number which can be portrayed as an oblong of dots. Note that what I have translated as 'oblong' numbers are always 'heteromecic'—that is, their sides differ by 1: 6 is 3x2, 12 is 4x3, and so on. Note also that any oblong number is the sum of two equal triangular numbers, and that oblong numbers are formed by the addition of any number of successive even numbers in the sequence of natural numbers (see also under *Gnomon*): 2+4=6, 2+4+6=12, etc.

Odd: A number which can be divided only into two unequal parts, of which one is odd and the other even.

Odd-even: An even number which becomes odd when divided by some power of 2. Example: 24, successively divided into 12, 6, 3.

Over-perfect: A number which is less than the sum of its factors. Example: 12, whose factors (1, 2, 3, 4, 6) add up to 16.

Perfect: Strictly, a perfect (or 'complete') number is one which is equal to the sum of its factors. Example: 6, whose factors are 1, 2,

3. But numbers could also be called perfect in less strictly mathematical senses (see e.g. pp. 60-61.)

Plane: A number which can be portrayed as an array of evenly spaced dots in the shape of a plane figure. See: *Triangular, Square, Oblong, Polygonal.*

Polygonal: A number which can be portrayed as dots in the shape of a polygon. See also under *Gnomon.*

Prime and incomposite: A number which can be measured or factored only by 1 and by itself. Earlier Greek mathematicians regarded 2 as prime, as we do today; but for later writers this category of number was one of the three categories of odd number (see also: *Secondary, Mixed*), to balance the three categories of even number (see: *Even-times-even, Even-odd, Odd-even*).

Rectilinear: see *Linear.*

Recurrent: see *Spherical.*

Scalene: A solid number which is the product of three unequal numbers. Example: 64, seen as the product of 2x4x8.

Secondary and composite: To earlier Greek mathematicians, a composite number is any number which is not prime. To later mathematicians, secondary and composite numbers were one of the three classes of odd number (see under *Prime*): they are odd numbers whose factors are both odd and prime. Example: 15, whose factors are 3 and 5.

Side: A number considered as the side of a plane or solid figured number. Hence 'side' has sometimes been translated as 'square root' (where it is the side of a square) and 'factor' (where it is the side of an oblong). Side numbers are often paired with diagonal numbers, because the Pythagoreans used the relation between the side and the diagonal of a square to prove the irrationality of √2, and to find successive approximations to $\sqrt{2}$.

Solid: A number which can be portrayed as a three-dimensional array of evenly spaced dots. See: *Cube, Scalene.*

Spherical: A cube number whose last digit is the same as the last digit of the side number. Also called 'recurrent.' So a spherical number is bound to end in 1, 5 or 6. Examples: 216 (6^3), 1331 (11^3).

Square: A number which can be portrayed as a square of evenly spaced dots. These are the familiar square numbers. Also called 'equal-times-equal.' Note that square numbers are formed by the addition of any number of successive odd numbers in the sequence of natural numbers (see also under *Gnomon*): 1+3=4, 1+3+5=9, etc. See also: *Circular.*

Submultiple: The opposite to a multiple, i.e. a number which cannot be factorized (and is therefore prime), but which is a factor of some other number.

Triangular: A number which can be portrayed as a triangle of evenly spaced dots. Note than any triangular number is half an oblong number, and that triangular numbers are formed by the addition of any numbers of successive terms in the sequence of natural numbers: 1+2=3, 1+2+3=6, etc.

B. Other Terms

Color: Surface, or surface area.

Double sesquitertian: The ratio 7:3, because it contains 3 twice, with a third left over. See also: *Sesquitertian.*

Gnomon: Originally, a carpenter's square (L-shaped). In mathematics, given the archaic practice of portraying numbers as arrays of dots, this shape delineates the sequence of odd or even numbers which form, respectively, squares or oblongs:

However, while in these cases the original shape of the carpenter's tool is preserved, the same cannot be said for the gnomons of polygonal numbers. Here, for example, are the successive pentagonal numbers 1, 5 12, with their gnomons of 4 and 7:

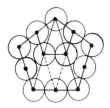

Sesquialter: The ratio 3:2, which in music measures the concord of a fifth.

Sesquioctave: The ratio 9:8, which in music is a whole tone.

Sesquitertian: The ratio 4:3, which in music measures the concord of a fourth.

Subcontrary: Originally used to describe the harmonic mean, as opposed to the arithmetic and geometric means. Later, these three were taken as the standards, and three of the further seven means which were distinguished were called 'subcontrary' (opposed)— one to the harmonic, the other two to the geometric. Example: in the proportion a:b:c, b is the geometric mean if $(c-b)/(b-a)=b/a$ (e.g. 1, 2, 4). However, in the proportion a:b:c, b is the 'fifth' mean, and subcontrary to the geometric if $(b-a)/(c-b)=b/a$ (e.g. 2, 4, 5).

Subsesquialter: The inverse of the sesquialter, i.e. the ratio 2:3.

Tetraktys: The decad considered as the sum of the first four numbers, and usually portrayed as a triangular number:

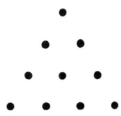

The tetraktys was held in great reverence by the Pythagoreans, and was their basic model or map of how things are. Since the tetraktys contains all the numbers from 1 to 10, in a sense the whole of *The Theology of Arithmetic* is about the tetraktys. Many of the particular reasons why the tetraktys was so admired are given in the sections of the treatise which are devoted to the tetrad and the decad.

Biography

Many of the people mentioned in the treatise occur only incidentally, but it may be as well for the reader to know at least their dates. Further information may be found in the *Oxford Classical Dictionary* or (better, but in German) Pauly-Wissowa, *Real-Encyclopädie.*

Anacreon: lyric poet, sixth century B.C.

Anatolius: Christian arithmologist, third century A.D.

Anaxagoras: philosopher, fifth century B.C.

Androcydes: Pythagorean, possibly late fourth century B.C.

Aristaeus: Pythagoras' successor as head of the school

Aristoxenus: musicologist and philosopher, fourth century B.C.

Cambyses: King of Persia, 530-522 B.C.

Cleinias: Pythagorean, contemporary with Plato

Diocles: physician, fourth century B.C.

Empedocles: philosopher-mystic, fifth century B.C.

Eratosthenes: scientific and literary polymath, third century B.C.

Eubulides: Pythagorean, date unknown

Euripides: playwright, fifth century B.C.

Harpagus: Persian commander, sixth century B.C.

Hesiod: epic poet, *c.* 700 B.C.

Hippobotus: biographer of philosophers, late third century B.C.

Hippocrates: physician, fifth century B.C.

Homer: epic poet, *c.* 750 B.C.

Hostanes: teacher of Zoroaster

Linus: Pythagorean, date unknown

Megillus: arithmologist, date unknown

Neanthes: historian, third century B.C.

Nicomachus: Neopythagorean, late first and early second centuries A.D.

Orpheus: legendary mystic and poet

Parmenides: philosopher, fifth century B.C.

Philolaus: Pythagorean, fifth century B.C.

Plato: philosopher, late fifth and early fourth centuries B.C.

Polycrates: tyrant of Samos, late sixth century B.C.

Prorus: early Pythagorean

Pythagoras: arithmological philosopher-mystic, sixth century B.C.

Solon: Athenian statesman, poet and sage, late seventh and early sixth centuries B.C.

Speusippus: Plato's nephew and successor as head of the Academy

Strato: third head of Aristotle's school of philosophy, late fourth and early third centuries B.C.

Xenocrates: Platonist, third head of the Academy, fourth century B.C.

Xenophanes: philosopher and lyric poet, sixth century B.C.

Zoroaster: founder of Zoroastrian religion, sixth century B.C.

A Kairos Book

This is a translation commissioned by Kairos, which is a registered British Charity established to promote, through education, research and publication, the study of the perennial wisdom of humanity, whose goal is to recognize the inherent unity of the spiritual and natural worlds.

Studies into this ancient body of wisdom can provide us with an invaluable perspective that links modern scientific reality and traditional spiritual reality into a true science of life that can direct us towards the fulfillment of peace and harmony on Earth. This sacred science recognizes the principle of Unity, the knowledge that the universe is an integral being, and that our goal in life is to realize the uniqueness of each aspect of life within the unified whole of existence.

Further information may be had by writing:

KAIROS
21 BROOMHOUSE ROAD
LONDON SW6 3QU
UK
Registered charity no. 274967

or in North America

KAIROS
c/o D. YARBOROUGH
3100 MONTICELLO
DALLAS, TEXAS 75205
USA

Bibliography

I hope that classical scholars, as well as other interested readers, will use this volume; but classical scholars know where to go to find their technical works (I have used Klein's bibliography on pp. xviii-xxiii of his preface to de Falco's Teubner text for works up to the early 1970s, and otherwise *L'Année Philologique*). This bibliography is therefore restricted to relevant works which, while they may require some concentration, are generally both accessible and valuable to a Greekless, non-specialist reader.

Adam, J., *The Nuptial Number of Plato,* Cambridge University Press, 1891; repr. Wellingborough, Kairos/Thorsons, 1985.

Armstrong, A.H. (ed.), *The Cambridge History of Later Greek and Early Medieval Philosophy,* Cambridge University Press, 1967.

Burkert, W., *Lore and Science in Ancient Pythagoreanism,* Harvard University Press, 1972.

Cornford, F.M., *Plato's Cosmology,* London, Routledge & Kegan Paul, 1937.

Cumont, F., *Astrology and Religion Among the Greeks and Romans,* New York, 1912; repr. New York, Dover, 1960.

Demos, R., *The Philosophy of Plato,* London, Charles Scribner's Sons, 1939.

Dicks, D.R., *Early Greek Astronomy to Aristotle,* London, Thames and Hudson, 1970.

Dillon, J., *The Middle Platonists,* London, Duckworth, 1977.

Farrington, B., *Science in Antiquity,* Oxford University Press, 1969.

Findlay, J.N., *Plato: The Written and Unwritten Doctrines*, London, Routledge & Kegan Paul,1974.

Flegg, G., *Numbers: Their History and Meaning*, London, André Deutsch, 1983.

Friedländer, P., *Plato: An Introduction*, Princeton University Press, 1958.

Grant, F.C., *Hellenistic Religions*, Indianapolis, Bobbs-Merrill, 1953.

Guthrie, K.S., *The Pythagorean Sourcebook and Library*, New York, Platonist Press,1919; expanded and revised edition, Grand Rapids, Phanes Press, 1987.

Guthrie, W.K.C., *The Greeks and Their Gods*, London, Methuen, 1950.
——*A History of Greek Philosophy*, Volume I: *The Earlier Presocratics and the Pythagoreans*, Cambridge University Press, 1971.

Heath, T.L., *Aristarchus of Samos: The Ancient Copernicus*, Oxford University Press, 1913.
—— *A History of Greek Mathematics*, 2 volumes, Oxford University Press, 1921; repr. New York, Dover, 1981.

Kirk, G.S., Raven, J.E., and Schofield, M., *The Presocratic Philosophers*, 2nd ed., Cambridge University Press, 1983.

Lloyd, G.E.R., *Early Greek Science : Thales to Aristotle*, London, Chatto & Windus, 1970.
——*Greek Science After Aristotle*, London, Chatto & Windus, 1973.

Long, A.A., *Hellenistic Philosophy*, London, Duckworth, 1974.

Luck, G., *Arcana Mundi: Magic and the Occult in the Greek and*

Roman World, Baltimore, Johns Hopkins University Press, 1985.

Michaelides, S., *The Music of Ancient Greece: An Encyclopedia*, London, Faber and Faber, 1978.

Neugebauer, O.E., *The Exact Sciences in Antiquity*, Princeton University Press, 1951.

Nicomachus of Gerasa, *Introduction to Arithmetic*, translated by M.L. D'Ooge, introduction by F.E. Robbins and L.C. Karpinski, New York, Macmillan, 1926.

Philip, J.A., *Pythagoras and Early Pythagoreanism*, Toronto, University of Toronto Press, 1966.

Phillips, E.D., *Greek Medicine*, London, Thames and Hudson, 1973.

Plotinus, *The Enneads*, translated by S. Mackenna, revised by B.S. Page, London, Faber and Faber, 1956.

Proclus, *The Elements of Theology*, ed. E.R. Dodds, 2nd ed., Oxford University Press, 1963.

Rose, H.J., *A Handbook of Greek Mythology*, Methuen, 1928.

Sambursky, S., *The Physical World of the Greeks*, London, Routledge & Kegan Paul, 1956.

Taylor, T., *The Theoretic Arithmetic of the Pythagoreans*, London, 1816; repr. York Beach, Maine, Samuel Weiser, 1972.

Theon of Smyrna, *Mathematics Useful for Understanding Plato*, trans. R. and D. Lawlor, San Diego, Wizards Bookshelf, 1979.

Thesleff, H., *An Introduction to the Pythagorean Writings of the Hellenistic Period*, Åbo, Åbo Academy, 1961.

Thomas, I., *Greek Mathematical Works*, 2 volumes, Harvard University Press, 1939 and 1941.

Wallis, R.T., *Neoplatonism*, London, Duckworth, 1972.

PHANES PRESS both publishes and distributes many fine books which relate to the philosophical, religious and spiritual traditions of the Western world. To obtain a copy of our current catalogue, please write:

PHANES PRESS
PO BOX 6114
GRAND RAPIDS, MI 49516
USA